A **Mindset** for **Learning**

Teaching the Traits of **Joyful, Independent Growth**

A **Mindset** for **Learning**

Teaching the Traits of **Joyful, Independent Growth**

Kristine **Mraz** Christine **Hertz**

HEINEMANN
Portsmouth, NH

Heinemann
361 Hanover Street
Portsmouth, NH 03801–3912
www.heinemann.com

Offices and agents throughout the world

Library of Congress Cataloging-in-Publication Data
Mraz, Kristine.
A mindset for learning : teaching the traits of joyful, independent growth / Kristine Mraz and Christine Hertz.
pages cm
Includes bibliographical references.
ISBN 978-0-325-06288-4
1. Elementary school teaching. 2. Moral education (Elementary). I. Hertz, Christine. II. Title.
LB1555.M77 2015
372.1102—dc23 2015014306

Editor: Zoë Ryder White
Production: Hilary Goff
Cover design: Monica Ann Crigler
Interior design: Shawn Girsberger
Typesetter: Shawn Girsberger
Manufacturing: Steve Bernier

Printed in the United States of America on acid-free paper
19 18 17 16 EBM 5

For my parents,
for showing me how to stay forever young.

With love, CEH

For Geoff,
who fixed my heart,
and
for Grace,
who will fix the world.

With Love, KMM

Contents

Acknowledgments

Each friend represents a world in us, a world possibly not born until they arrive, and it is only by this meeting that a new world is born.

—ANAÏS NIN, *The Diary of Anaïs Nin, Vol. 1: 1931–1934*

This book began first as a conversation about a small wish, or dream, that we could become the kind of teachers who would stand for the things that mattered to us, no matter the obstacles. From that first conversation to this moment, where you, our reader, are reading these words, we have found so many others to stand with us. We believe that an educational system that does not value children's voices, hearts, and minds is inherently flawed. We believe that the best education is one through which children recognize their own power and potential and their ultimate duty to make the world around them a better place. We believe teachers have the power to build classrooms of energized, engaged, and joyful learning, classrooms where we value who each child is as much as we value what the child knows on any assessment. It is with the deepest gratitude that we thank the people who pushed us, supported us, inspired us, and challenged us and who, most of all, stand right alongside with us.

First and foremost, we would like to thank the teachers and administrators who built the ecosystems that have helped us outgrow ourselves. We admire our administrators' fearless leadership, thoughtful feedback, and open-door policies. These leaders have built schools of growth and innovation because they have never stopped growing and innovating. Within our schools, we have been lucky enough to find kindred teaching spirits, who have pushed us to think more boldly; this book would not have existed without them. It is with love, pride, and no small amount of respect that we thank Kathryn Cazes, Mollie Gaffney-Smith, Katie Lee, Valerie Geschwind, and Megan Maynard Jacob. You humble us with your talent for innovation, your care for children, and your joy.

The final component in our ecosystems is among the most important: our students. This book would not have been possible without our incredible students and their families. We thank them from the bottom of our hearts for their honesty, bravery, and constant feedback. Not a day goes by that we are not amazed at the power and potential in each of our students and the support and grace of the families we work with daily.

In truth, this book might have just stayed a conversation, if not for our incredible team at Heinemann. We would like to extend our gratitude to our production editor, Hilary Goff, who answered every question with a smile and kept us running right on schedule. We'd also like to thank our copyeditor, Elizabeth Tripp, for smoothing our words and reducing our exclamation marks down from every sentence to only every third or so. Monica Crigler is responsible for our beautiful cover and lovely layout—thank you for capturing the heart of our book in images. Finally, our thanks to Kiele Raymond, our editorial coordinator, for her gentle nudges and eagle eyes.

And to our editor, Zoë Ryder White: there are no words to encompass our thanks, but we will try. Zoë's compassion, humor, precise feedback, and thoughtful questions were the guideposts that brought this book to life. Zoë is all you could ask for in a mentor, teacher, and friend. Compassionate, brilliant, reflective, and fearless, she is the model we aim to live up to, one day. For Zoë, a million thanks for unmixing our metaphors, unearthing our points, and correcting our *Sound of Music* song lyrics, all while encouraging us to be braver, more precise, and constantly growing. Thank you for believing in us and for helping us to become better writers, better thinkers, and better people.

Christine would like to begin by thanking Kristi, her coauthor, her friend. Kristi's remarkable talent and intelligence are matched only by her heart and her vision for what is possible in this world. Kristi has a gift for inspiring everyone she interacts with to be the very best versions of themselves. Kristi, thank you for making me think deeply, laugh regularly, and expand my belief of what is possible. Christine would also like to thank her family and friends. She is especially grateful for each time they nudged her just a teeny bit outside her comfort zone and helped her discover that often it's the leaps of faith that get her to the best parts of life. Thank you for keeping the home fires burning.

Kristi would first like to thank her amazing coauthor, Christine. There are people you meet who fit with you like a puzzle piece, and you realize together you are more than you were alone. Sharing a friendship with Christine is like a getting a master's degree in being a better human. I am eternally grateful for her belief in children, her ability to reflect and be thoughtful, and her generosity with her brilliance. The world is better for having her in it. Kristi would also like to thank her husband, Geoff. He is brave and compassionate, hardworking and thoughtful, brilliant and goofy. He is, in short, her inspiration for nearly everything worth doing. Thank you, Geoff, for so many years of thoughtful conversation, unwavering kindness, and constant joy.

Introduction

Start at the Very Beginning (a Very Good Place to Start)

It is September in a New York City kindergarten and the fire alarm is going off for a drill for the very first time. Reactions from the group of four- and five-year-olds are mixed. Michael throws up immediately. Dan and Adrian yell, "Gross!"

Gabriel yells, "Fire!" and runs at full speed to the door, followed closely on his heels by two or three others.

Sophia, Kate, and Erin don't appear to have noticed the bright flashing lights or the loud beeping and don't bother to look up from their drawings.

We, Christine and Kristi, look at each other, wide-eyed, and share our first simultaneous thought, "Oh, please, God, no." A fire drill on the third day of kindergarten. We haven't even had an opportunity to walk in a line yet.

Quickly, quickly, we usher the twenty-six children to the door. Like kittens, as soon as one reaches the line, two others find something vastly interesting in a different direction. Christine keeps the back of the line moving forward as Kristi keeps the lead moving in the right direction. It looks promising; it looks like K-309 will make it out of the sch—

Bam! *Claire falls down—Claire of the "bandages for everything" lifestyle—and she refuses to get up. Christine scoops her up and we keep moving and almost reach the door. . . .*

Alex has lost a shoe. How? Why? How? There is no time to ponder the near impossibility that a shoe could be lost in the thirty feet the class has walked. We have one goal: the door. We finally emerge on the sidewalk outside of the school like victims of a shipwreck. Children crying, shoes lost, wild looks in Kristi's and Christine's eyes. Christine sets the sniffling Claire down on the sidewalk and gazes at the children in her immediate vicinity. Amelia, the ineffably resilient and intrepid Amelia, turns to her, smiles, and says, "That was an adventure, right?!"

In the face of something brand-new, something potentially very scary for a child who has never been to school, Amelia has seen adventure, and possibility, and, above all, a reason to smile.

It is our deepest wish to build classrooms of risk and resilience so that all children, not just the Amelias of the world, have an opportunity to live bigger and more bravely in the world. To live, and to engage, with hope and joy.

Before we begin this journey together, there is a small matter that must be cleared up: who are *we*, exactly? Well, there is you, the reader, and there is us, the authors, Kristi Mraz and Christine Hertz. The authors' part of the relationship began a few years ago, when Christine was completing an action research project around metacognition and play in Kristi's kindergarten classroom. We became fast friends and educational allies, the kind of partners who play a version of the "Yes, and . . ." improv game, but with instruction. "What if we themed the reading work to *Star Wars*?!" one of us asked, and the other answered, "Yes, and . . . what if the kids got Yoda ears when they mastered one strategy and could teach it to other kids?!"

The unifying thread of our relationship is our desire to exist within the parameters of the punctuation sequence *?!*—curiosity coupled with excitement, wonder matched with joy. But as Christine went back to work in her third-grade classroom in Vermont, and Kristi continued her life as a kindergarten teacher in New York City, we found ourselves struggling to maintain that vision in the increased demand of [*thunderclaps*] R-I-G-O-R [*thunderclaps*] that has accompanied the dialogue around the Common Core State Standards.

What is rigor exactly? What does "college and career ready" really mean?

Is it five-year-olds sitting silently for forty minutes? Is it second graders breaking down the themes in *War and Peace*? Is it fifth graders closely reading a three-hundred-page book for the entire year? The answer is no. Nor is rigor a teacher dumping information into an empty vessel. It is not passive learning. Rigor is not fourth graders staring at a Shakespearean sonnet while their teacher deconstructs its symbolism. Nor is rigor first graders memorizing all of their addition and subtraction facts without developing any number sense. Rigor is not a gold "Common Core Aligned!" sticker on the front of a prepackaged curriculum. It is not accepting the status quo. So what is it?

Rigor is active. Rigor is passionate. Rigor is about who we are as much as what we know. As teachers, we help shape the future with every child that walks through our doors. We cannot let fear of benchmarks stand in the way of helping children find their value and their voice. What does it matter if a child can read on level if that same child does not believe she has power and agency? A child in passive receipt of learning will be in passive receipt of life. It is our rally cry that we create schools of joy and change. But how? How does one set the conditions for developmentally appropriate, child-centered, playful rigor?! Rigor that helps a student become a better person, not just a higher number on a state test? How do we ensure the child is not lost in the quest for standards while still reaching those standards? How do we keep the *kids* in the curriculum? And how do we make the goal for the children's future be not just "college and career ready" but "love, life, and agents of change ready"?

Finding the right questions sent us on a quest that continues in this book and with you, our reader, the final component of our *we*. So who are we, exactly? We are educators who believe in passionate and playful practice. We are people who honor childhood and joy. We see our debt to the children before us but also to the world that they will help create. We value inquiry and exploration. We are learners, we are seekers, we are teachers.

The Journey of a Thousand Miles Begins with a Single Book

Kristi was on a Twitter chat one July night in 2013 when she saw a tweet by Daniel Pink, author of *Drive* and *A Whole New Mind*, encouraging teachers to read the book *Mindset*, by Carol Dweck (2007). Curious, Kristi downloaded the book and consumed it over a few nights. Christine, already familiar with the book, reread it, and we began talking. The central thesis of *Mindset* is that there are two ways people think about themselves and the world:

1. **Fixed Mindset**: When you think about yourself and the world with a fixed mindset, you believe that your traits, habits, personality, skills, and so on are fixed and immovable. You are smart or dumb, athletic or clumsy, artistic or not. There is nothing you can do to change these traits. For this reason, effort is not particularly valued. Why try if you know you are dumb? Likewise, failure is a terrifying prospect. If you fail, does that mean you were never smart in the first place?
2. **Growth Mindset**: When you think about yourself and the world with a growth mindset, you believe that your traits, habits, personality, skills, and so on are growing and changing. You are not smart or dumb, athletic or clumsy, artistic or not. You are constantly in progress. Effort is the linchpin of this mindset: who knows how far you will go if you try? And failures

> are feedback. They may still hurt, but they are not endpoints; they are sign-posts on ways to proceed in the future.

This dichotomy of mindsets launched us into action. Throughout *Mindset*, we found examples of how people with growth mindsets were happier, more successful, more apt to create lasting change in themselves and in the world. What more could we want for ourselves and our students? Couldn't this be the start of an answer to what "college and career ready" means, an answer that we could believe in? Yes, we want our students to be able to read critically, to solve complex problems, and to write effectively. But more importantly, we want our students to leverage those skills to take on challenges with zeal and to see themselves not as static test scores that are either "college or career ready" or not but rather as ever-evolving and powerful agents of change, both for themselves and for their world. Could this be the new way we think about rigor in the classroom? Not as the work you do, but *how* you do the work you do, who you are, and what you believe about yourself and others? Carol Dweck's momentous book fired our engines, and our quest began. We hopped from self-help books to neurology texts, asking ourselves, "What can we do to help our children become the best people they can be, to then make the best world they can?"

A Constellation of Stances for an Energized and Engaged Learning Community

Everything we read on the quest to strive for joyful, successful, and powerful learning in our classrooms converged on a single idea (see Appendix A and the "Works Cited" section for a list of exactly what we read). There are habits or stances that we can build in ourselves that will make us more successful and happier. Just as a ready stance in baseball (knees bent, glove out, eyes on the ball) makes us more likely to catch a ball if it happens our way, the ready positions in our brains dictate how we react to challenges and new events. Variations on the same idea came up again and again: resilience, flexibility, optimism, empathy, persistence, grit, organization. It seemed that everywhere we looked, everyone was talking about the same thing we were thinking about. Even the National Council of the Teachers of English has published its own list of stances, or habits, that help learners achieve the most that they can (to see the list, go to http://wpacouncil.org/files/framework-for-success-postsecondary-writing.pdf).

We agreed as we pondered the lists that this all sounded like a great way to live in the world. Yet in all of this reading, we were missing the *how*. How does one teach children to be these things? So we did what we always do: we began a game of "Yes, and . . .," which brought us to the very book you hold in your hands. We did not invent the stances or habits, nor did we invent the different techniques we suggest for teaching them; however, we found a playful way to combine parts of our day and the elements that make up successful people to change the tone and talk in our classrooms.

We started focusing on *persistence* with our kindergarten and third-grade students and then quickly realized that persistence in isolation has its limitations. We asked ourselves, "How much are our students growing by building the exact same block tower over and over again, only to watch it continually fall? Or by using the same word-attack strategy over and over again with no luck?" At what point is persistence for the sake of persistence ineffective? Then we asked ourselves, "What should we teach our students to do when persistence alone doesn't work? What else could help our students take risks and overcome challenges?" So we read more and talked more to our colleagues and expanded our conversations with students to include *flexibility* and then *resilience*. Soon we added in *optimism*, and then we realized none of these talks would be worth it without also having conversations around *empathy* and community (for more on these stances, see Chapter 3). We began to call this collection a *constellation of stances* because one stance by itself is not nearly as powerful as its interplay with the others. And so, over the course of two classrooms and two years, we began to focus our teaching on:

- empathy
- optimism
- resilience
- persistence
- and flexibility.

And realized, only when you embrace all of these stances do you truly begin to feel the limitless possibility of life, learning, and yourself (see Figure I.1).

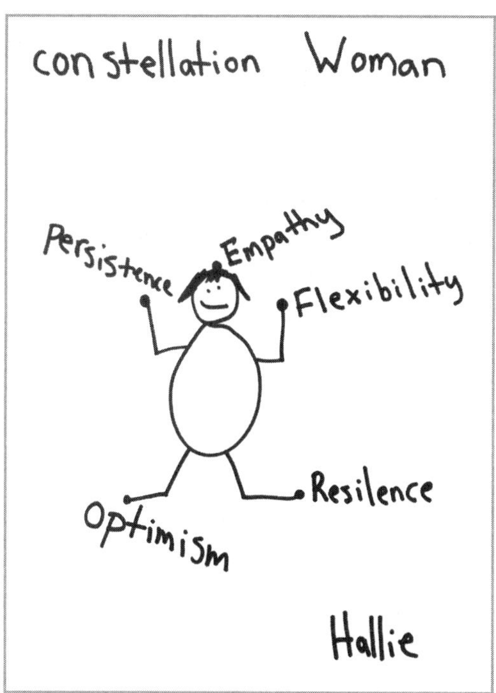

Figure I.1 Christine's Student's Illustration of the Constellation of Stances

As we experimented in our own classrooms and others, read more, and talked with colleagues, we began to realize that the stances we were working on were akin to the needs of saltwater fish: they need a certain pH to thrive; they need a community ecosystem that values and fosters their development. In all the energized and engaged classrooms we've worked in, we've found that certain elements repeated themselves, such as workshop teaching structures and a playful, joyful approach to teaching and learning (see Chapter 1 for more on these essential elements).

Take a Leap of Faith

In her book *Daring Greatly*, Brené Brown draws upon Theodore Roosevelt's famous speech, challenging us to "walk into the arena, whatever it may be . . . with courage and the willingness to engage" (2012, 2). She continues, "Rather than sitting on the sidelines and hurling judgment and advice, we must dare to show up and let ourselves be seen. This is vulnerability. This is daring greatly." As teachers, we know well that life would be easier outside the arena. Outside the arena, we can deliver the curriculum as it is handed down to us. We can push and pull our students toward academic benchmarks and teach them how to "do" school. We can pack up our bags at the end of the day and say, "Good enough." Life is safer and easier outside the arena.

But, as teachers, we also know in our hearts that our place is actually inside the arena. Inside the arena, we advocate passionately for what is best for our students while helping them develop their own agency and voice. We do all we can to dodge the judgments that are hurled at us, and we use our best judgment to help our students thrive. Inside the arena is where we do our most important work—our work as teachers is to dare greatly and to teach our children to do the same.

Thousands of miles later—or at least thousands of conversations, trials, mistakes, brainstorms, and "ahas" later—we invite you to take up your own journey. Redefine rigor in your classroom. Reintroduce joy, creativity, and play. Take risks. Embrace failure wholeheartedly. Grow as a teacher. As you go forward from this point on, know that you are not standing alone. We—the collective we—are standing, teaching, and learning side by side. And, together, we will help your students become the brave, engaged, energized learners and people we need them to be.

Bridging from Theory to Practice: How to Use This Book

Christine was flipping through a cooking magazine when a glossy photo and catchy title caught her eye: "Okra—the Power of the Pods." Curious, she read on. Before the recipes, the article discussed a little bit about the health benefits, the heritage, and even the argument for okra. Cooking magazines have a knack for getting you to try something new; they justify *why* you would want to try it and then clearly lay out *how* you could do it.

We have found that the best books for educators have something in common: they balance theory and research (the what and the why) with practice (the how). Such books engage us intellectually, change our thinking, and then give us direct, practical ideas for classroom implementation. Our hope is that this book achieves such a balance.

Chapter 1 will provide you with a field guide to your classroom, and Chapter 2 will act as a field guide to your students, inviting you to think carefully about each individual student and your class as a whole.

The remaining chapters are designed to work in pairs. The first chapter in a pair focuses on theory, relevancy, and research and the second focuses on application and practice. Our hope is that these chapter pairs will leave you both eager and prepared to start engaging with this work in your own classroom.

CHAPTER 1

Building a Classroom Ecosystem of Energy and Engagement

Growing up, Kristi had a goldfish named Harry. Harry lived with three other fish in a tank for years. One by one the other fish left their mortal coil until just Harry was left, and then a very peculiar thing happened. Harry started to grow and grow, despite having spent many years at the same size. You may have heard the phrase "goldfish grow to the size of their bowl," but you may not know it is literally true. A change of ecosystem can generate some surprising results.

Schools and classrooms have their own kinds of ecosystems. You just have to think back to the variety of teachers you experienced to feel the truth of that. One classroom might have made you feel like you could accomplish anything; others may have left you worried about straying from a straight and narrow path. We use the term *ecosystem* because it is not just one component that builds a successful classroom atmosphere, but many working in concert. After visiting classrooms, working with diverse groups of teachers, and experimenting in our own rooms, we have come to recognize a few conditions of ecosystems that support an energized and engaged learning community. Let's call it an ecosystem of joyful effort.

Building a Community of Support and Encouragement

> *A child does not just become a thinker and a problem solver; she becomes a special kind of thinker, rememberer, listener, and communicator, which is a reflection of the social context.*
>
> —ELENA BODROVA AND DEBORAH LEONG, *Tools of the Mind*

Self-regulation, persistence, tenacity. Depending on context, these stances can fuel very different outcomes. When used in connection with a single-minded pursuit of success, expertise, or achievement, these words evoke competitive spirit, domination, and even a kind of narcissism.

Yet these words can also name the fuel that resulted in successful fights for marriage equality, voting rights, and equal pay for equal work. We did not begin to study these ideas so that all of our students would have the kind of ruthless determination needed to run Wall Street. Rather, we asked ourselves, "What kind of people are the happiest, most creative, and most productive? What end should grit, persistence, and tenacity serve—individual gain or community good?" To our thinking, stances, like grit, are not inherently bad or good; they are neutral, but it is the end they serve that matters. To this point, we value and teach into a community and global view. Most early childhood and elementary school teachers speak passionately about building community in the beginning of the year, but what *kind* of community we build is a bigger question.

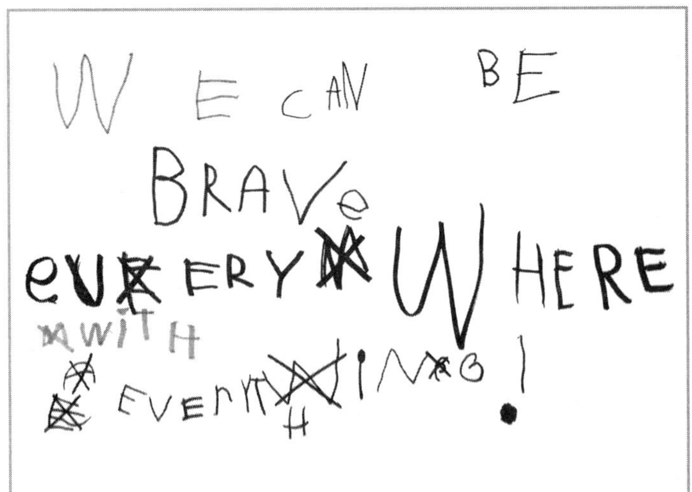

FIGURE 1.1 "We Can Be Brave" Sign Outside a Kindergarten Classroom

Paul Tough (2012) makes much of the infamous "marshmallow test," where very young children were given the choice of receiving one marshmallow in the moment or two if they could delay gratification. Those children who were able to wait longer proved to be more successful later in life. Yet we read a curious caveat about the same "marshmallow test" in Sarah Lewis' book *The Rise* (2014). There was a follow-up study to the marshmallow test where the person in charge of giving the marshmallows was proven reliable or unreliable before the child was given the option of receiving one marshmallow immediately or two if he or she could wait. Children who found the provider unreliable were, wisely, less likely to wait. What does this tell us? That a child's self-control, tenacity, and persistence are influenced first by their environment and the reliability and consistency of their caregivers. If we want to build a community of persistence, joy, resilience, flexibility, and empathy, we must first *be* all of those things, and be *reliable* in those things.

We believe that a teacher works to become an invisible force in the classroom, but a force nonetheless. In their book *Tools of The Mind*, Elena Bodrova and Deborah Leong (2007) underscore how influential a teacher is in communicating not only information but also ways of thinking and being. They say a "teacher's ideas mediate what and how the child will learn; they act as a filter in a sense, determining which ideas the children will learn" (9). Implicitly, or explicitly, teachers select certain things to highlight and certain things to ignore. In this way we can build a community that highlights being smart or one that values effort and flexibility. A teacher can direct the way a community works in the intentional celebration of specific actions and words of its members.

In *Visible Learners* (Krechevsky et al. 2013), Melissa Tonachel, a kindergarten and first-grade teacher, describes how children in her class regularly talk about how they are inspired by each other's work. Tonachel offers some questions, phrases, and vocabulary that help develop this sense of collaboration. She might ask: "Where did that idea come from?" or "How did you learn to do that?" or "What inspired you?" She then prompts children to notice, wonder, and hypothesize about how they are building on their classmates' ideas, work, or play (67). By highlighting and fostering such conversations, Tonachel builds an ecosystem that deeply values and holds high expectations for collaboration.

In the most engaged and energized classrooms we have worked in, we've seen teachers who set up systems where children were accountable to their community. They were owners of the materials and the space. This expectation of responsibility and ownership is as though the teacher is stating, "This space is ours, to use and to care for." There are simple ways to achieve this message; for example, you can

- provide community supplies
- generate classroom jobs
- invite students to label materials and supplies (see Figure 1.2).

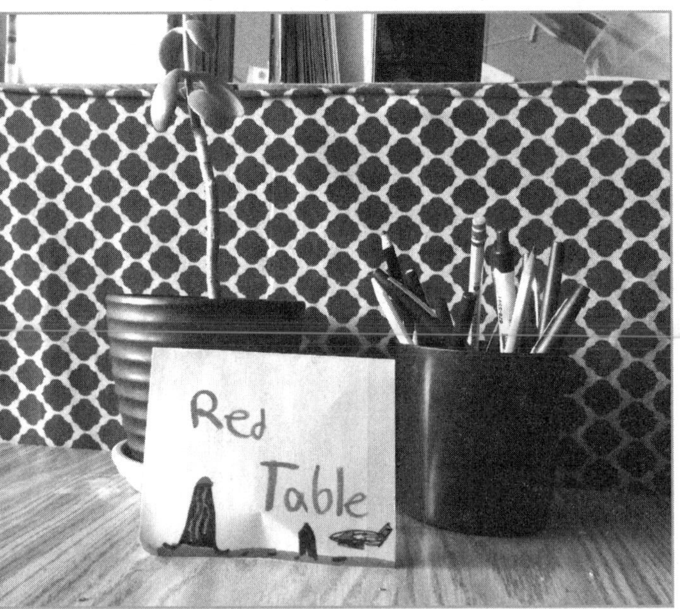

FIGURE 1.2 Student-Labeled Table

In addition to teaching students to care for a space, a teacher can set up the message that everyone in the classroom community should care about the people in the space just as much. There are a myriad of ways to do this, from holding community meetings to using problem-solving routines (see Figure 1.3).

In *Choice Words*, Peter Johnston (2004) highlights how a teacher's language—all of the things he says and doesn't say—has a profound effect on the ecosystem of the classroom. "Although language operates within relationships," he writes, "language practices also influence relationships among people and, consequently, the ways they think about themselves and each other" (9). A teacher's language directly impacts children's learning, identity, and agency in the classroom. (For more on Peter Johnston's work on language, see Chapters 11 and 12.) What is essential is a teacher's awareness of the values she communicates to her classroom community through her own words and deeds and in her celebrations of others'. As children learn what the teacher values, they often grow to value it too. Working to make a community a positive, respectful, and joyful place for all its members is at the core of building an energized and engaged classroom. (See Appendix A for more resources about the teacher's role in building the classroom culture.)

Teaching and Learning Through Play

> *It is becoming increasingly clear through research on the brain, as well as in other areas of study, that childhood needs play. Play acts as a forward feed mechanism into courageous, creative, rigorous thinking in adulthood.*
>
> —TINA BRUCE, "IN PRAISE OF INSPIRED AND INSPIRING TEACHERS"

In her beautiful treatise on overcoming failure, *The Rise*, Sarah Lewis (2014) relates the details of an experiment around the presentation of a toy. In it, the researchers

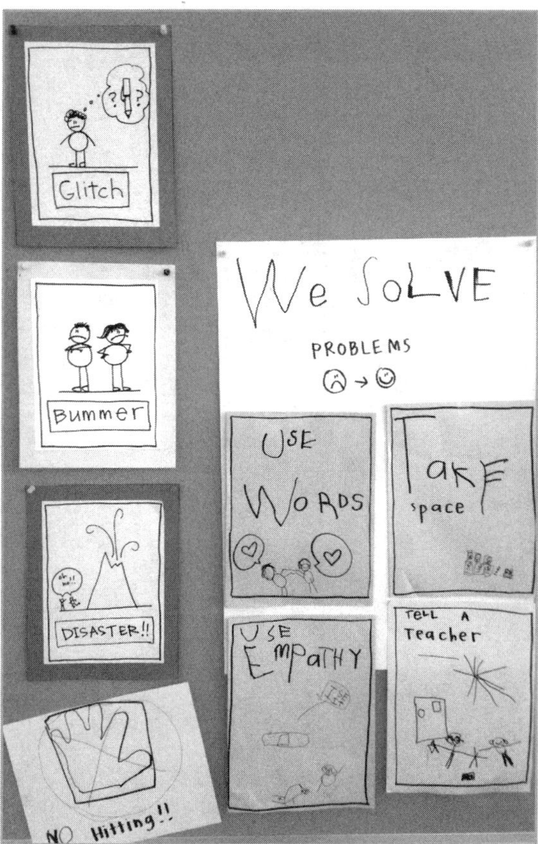

FIGURE 1.3 An Example of a Problem-solving Routine

presented two groups of children with the same toy in two different ways. One group learned about the toy through direct instruction: this is the toy; this is how it works. The second group was given the toy with no direction and allowed instead to freely play with it. Intuitively, you may already suspect the outcome of this experiment: researchers found that the children who were allowed to explore the toy through play had greater curiosity, engagement, and stamina. They discovered hidden features on the toy that the direct-instruction group overlooked, they played longer, and they worked more collaboratively (158). This is not to say that there is not a place for direct instruction in the classroom or the world. However, direct instruction is not being squeezed out of classrooms to make room for more blocks. Sadly, it is the inverse of that statement that we have found to be true—play is continually overlooked as the most powerful place of learning for children. (See Figure 1.4.)

FIGURE 1.4 Science, Engineering, and Play at Work in Third Grade

We find the most powerful classroom cultures to be the ones that have rich opportunities for playful engagement. Play has a wide range of definitions—rough-and-tumble, fantasy, construction play, for starters—and all of them have a place in school. There is wild and raucous recess play, but there is also sustained and involved intentional play. Recess play exercises bodies and energizes spirits. The other kind of play may seem quieter, but it also works on mental dexterity, flexibility, and self-regulation (Bodrova and Leong 2007). This play can manifest as a choice time spent creating pretend worlds in the primary grades. It can manifest as inquiry-based play where children dramatize historical events or use blocks to build, and better understand, Roman civilization in upper-elementary classrooms.

Vygotsky himself argued that play was essential for children's development "and without it children did not develop the creativity, self regulation, and other underlying skills necessary for later development" (Bodrova and Leong 2007, 35). In fact, Sergio Pellis, a researcher at the University of Lethbridge in Alberta, Canada, has found that "the experience of play changes the connections of the neurons at the front end of your brain and without play experience, those neurons aren't changed" (Hamilton 2014). The wiring of the prefrontal cortex in childhood, Pellis says, prepares the brain for all of the executive functioning that will be required later.

In our own work in the classroom, we have found it essential to let children experiment with persistence, resilience, flexibility, and optimism in the times when they play (see Figure 1.5).

Play is innate to all animals and is suppressed only when danger is near at hand (Lewis 2014, 157). Consider the implications of that situation in reverse: If play stops because danger is near, does it mean that danger is near whenever play is not allowed? How will we foster a community of support and risk if we do not allow for play? Throughout this book you will find references to choice time, pretend play, and playful inquiry. (See Appendix A for more resources on play in the classroom.)

FIGURE 1.5 Optimism on the Playground

We believe that play not only aids in the development of academic skills but also in the development of who we are as people and as a community. (For every fifteen minutes of play, children tend to use a third of that time engaged in learning about mathematical, spatial, and architectural principles, according to Sarah Lewis [2014, 157–58].) Play can mean taking on a silly voice, dancing your way through transitions, and taking long, extended times to experiment with cardboard and tape, but in our classrooms, play really means that this space is safe for risks, for laughter, and for joy.

Understanding Development in Order to Create Just-Right Risks

> *We need to think about failure differently. I'm not the first to say that failure, when approached properly, can be an opportunity for growth. But the way most people interpret this assertion is that mistakes are a necessary evil. Mistakes aren't a necessary evil. They aren't evil at all. They are an inevitable consequence of doing something new (and, as such, should be seen as valuable; without them, we'd have no originality). And yet, even as I say that embracing failure is an important part of learning, I also acknowledge that acknowledging this truth is not enough.*
>
> *That's because failure is painful, and our feelings about this pain tend to screw up our understanding of its worth. To disentangle the good and the bad parts of failure, we have to recognize both the reality of the pain and the benefit of the resulting growth.*
>
> —EDWIN CATMULL AND AMY WALLACE, *Creativity, Inc.*

One of Vygotsky's most critical contributions to teaching was his understanding of a *zone of proximal development* for all developing minds. His emphasis on a zone, rather than a point, indicates there is range of knowing. What a child can do completely independently defines the beginning of the zone; what a child cannot do (even with scaffolds and prompts) is its end. Within the zone is a range of skills that a child is on the verge of being able to perform independently, but not quite yet. As a child masters a skill enough to take it on independently, the zone moves ahead a little bit more. When you have a deep understanding of a child's zone, you're like a personal trainer who knows when a client is ready to take on more weights. The skilled practitioner gives students just enough challenge to ensure successful struggle.

For a child to build positive neural connections between effort and outcome (see the box "A Very Basic Explanation of How the Brain Works," for more on the brain), she must experience a series of effortful events that result in successful outcomes. When a person is repeatedly given challenges outside her zone of development, like fifty-pound increases in weights at the gym, unhealthy associations begin to form: "No matter how hard I try, I will never be able to do . . ." or "I just cannot understand math." There is a way to learn almost anything, and it is not through effort alone, but rather through effort combined with a skilled and sensitive mentor who sets the learner up for just-right challenges.

Identifying a child's zone of proximal development is a lifelong study and is by no means easy. However, despite our limited knowledge, we can ensure no damage is done by always asking of a failure: was this a fault of the task being too hard or a fault of the setup not being supportive enough? It is not that we do not want children to experience failure, but that we want them to experience failure that has the potential to lead to success. We want them to experience failure that will prompt us

A VERY BASIC EXPLANATION OF HOW THE BRAIN WORKS

Understanding how the brain does what it does is not essential to becoming an energized and engaged learner; however, demystifying what is happening in these skulls of ours can help you visualize the changes the brain is capable of enacting.

Essentially the brain is made of many different types of cells. Among these cells are neurons. Neurons transmit messages between each other. Neurons that are stimulated together grow stronger connections, and the connections between neurons that are never (or rarely) stimulated together grow weaker and disappear (Ros and Farinella 2013). Conditioning, like Pavlov did with his dog, seeks to connect neurons intentionally, but repeated experience can do the same thing. Psychoanalyst Philippa Perry states it thusly: "Our experiences actually shape our brain matter" (2009, 6). Repeated experiences or frequent coincidences create strong connections between neurons. There is no time limit on when the brain can make these connections; neural pathways develop throughout all the years of one's life.

Some of these connections are healthy for our mental well-being—positive connections between effort and success, for example. These are connections we want to strengthen and maintain. Others are less healthy, like believing that failure makes people love you less. Healthy connections can be built from the start, by helping children connect and draw the best possible meanings from their own experiences. And connections that do not help us be our best selves and prohibit us from living fulfilled and happy lives can be rewired through intentional steps. The key takeaway? Your brain and the way you think about the world can change, and you can change it. (See Figure 1.6.)

FIGURE 1.6 A Student's Drawing of a Growing Brain

or them to ask, "So that didn't work, but what do I know now that will help me be successful next time?" and have the answer be instructional and useful to the children. In the words of Michael Schwalbe, in his article "Demystifying the Fear Factor in Failure," "Failure gives us valuable feedback that we use to address our regrettable actions and improve our situation in the future" (2013, 191). In the powerful and joyful classrooms we have worked in, teachers had an ever-changing sense of what a child was working toward, almost a minute-by-minute Doppler report on the intellectual and emotional weather of any given child. A strong sense of child development, a good curriculum, and careful kid watching are the tools any teacher can develop to tap into this responsive and flexible teaching. (For more on kid watching, see Chapter 2).

Inherent in this skill is the ability for a teacher to set up opportunities in any curricular area for children to be able to use flexibility, resilience, optimism, empathy, and persistence successfully, in ways that encourage them to find these tools useful and powerful. Understanding development and what a child is ready to try allows us to say, as John Hattie and Gregory Yates do in their book *Visible Learning and the Science of How We Learn*, "I know you can do these problems as they are just like the ones you did last week, but a bit harder" (2013, 221). Hattie and Yates acknowledge, "Encouragement works, not so much through persuasion, as it does through jogging the right memories at the right time" (221).

A culture that encourages risk requires a teacher who understands exactly what is at stake. How many of us have given up on something because we found it to be hard at the start: yoga, making popovers, building IKEA furniture? We cannot have children giving up on learning because we lack knowledge of just-right challenges and the individual needs and developmental paths of our students. That brings us to the importance of teaching within a workshop structure.

Personalizing Instruction Through Workshop Teaching Structures

> *Excellent teachers therefore need to understand thinking, realise how difficult many tasks are for beginners, and find ways to encourage students to build confidence and invest effort to learn various strategies to thus think and learn. It is less about the "knowledge" to be learnt but more about the ways to progress from not knowing to knowing. This means that many of us as learners need a trusting, fair and safe environment to acknowledge that we "do not know" and will make errors in learning. Such learning takes time, but one of the teacher's roles is to maximize the efficiency of the time available, to provide many opportunities to learn the same ideas over time, and to ensure time is spent on learning and not merely doing "something."*
>
> —JOHN HATTIE AND GREGORY YATES, *Visible Learning and the Science of How We Learn*

The workshop model of instruction can balance play and direct instruction, inquiry and scaffolded practice, creativity and choice, community and autonomy. It is a model that adapts to the very specific needs of the students. Workshops are drivers of growth, engagement, and joyful teaching and learning. While workshop teaching is most widely used in reading and writing (and rests on the foundation of the work of Donald Graves, Lucy Calkins, Katie Wood Ray, and many others), the model can also be a means to teach mathematics, science, and social studies and even to facilitate intentional play during choice time. (See Appendix A for more on workshop teaching.) No matter the academic context, the workshop model allows teachers to tweak their teaching to meet the needs of their students in several ways.

Each workshop begins with a focused lesson, where the teacher delivers direct instruction and provides an opportunity for guided practice. Next, students embark on independent work time while the teacher confers one-on-one, leads small groups, and supports partnerships. Finally, the workshop concludes by pulling the group back together and sharing some final bit of learning or growth from the day's work. All of these components offer opportunities for scaffolding, modeling, and inquiry in a variety of contexts, including whole-class, small-group and one-on-one instruction.

Any teacher who has implemented the workshop model knows that these ecosystems of learning do not just spring into place when you reach the appointed time in your daily schedule. They take time, careful planning, resources, a deep understanding of your content, and, possibly, a healthy dose of blood, sweat, and tears. When they do come together the result is magical—the energy and zest for learning in a workshop are unmatched, and as the cogs and gears of the workshop start humming, children gain more and more independence and autonomy in their own growth. (For more resources on building independence within a workshop teaching structure, see Appendix A.) It may not look like it in September, but with constant and consistent routines and scaffolds toward independence, by November, the workshop will be able to run whether the teacher is there or not.

One key to a successful workshop is the teacher's responsiveness to the needs of his students. This responsiveness affects the units of study you implement, the lessons you teach, your small groups, and your conferences. Sometimes responsiveness is carefully planned in advance, as when a teacher uses the formative assessments that are embedded in workshop instruction—conferences, running records, rubrics, and exit tasks—to tweak and change his teaching based on his students' needs. At other times, responsiveness happens in the moment, as when a teacher sits side by side with a child or a group of children, carefully observes them, and offers specific suggestions and feedback. These continuous feedback loops are one of the most important drivers of student growth (Hattie and Yates 2013) and work hand in hand with the gradual release model. Teachers scaffold students' learning with models, tools, and other supports just enough to create that just-right risk and then remove those scaffolds, always working toward independence and autonomy. If a child were a car, and the standards were stops along the road that needed to be reached, then persistence, resilience, flexibility, optimism, and empathy would be the gas that would help the child reach the signposts on his own. The teacher cannot be the tow truck that drags a child through each standard, *even if it gets him there faster*, but the teacher can be the gas station attendant or roadside assistant that provides fuel, feedback, and a reassuring pat on the back so the child can get there on his own . . . and keep going.

The same responsiveness that drives your students' academic growth will drive how they take on the stances of engaged and energized learners. Because workshops offer so many places to tuck in personalized teaching and learning, they are the perfect vehicle to teach, practice, and reinforce students' persistence, flexibility, optimism, resilience, and empathy. Imagine focused lessons on resilience in writing, small groups that focus on flexibility in math, and conferences that set persistence goals in reading. In *The Art of Teaching Writing*, Lucy Calkins wrote,

> the most creative environments in our society are not the kaleidoscopic environments in which everything is always changing and complex. They are, instead, the predictable and consistent ones—the scholar's library, the researcher's laboratory, the artist's studio. Each of these environments is deliberately predictable and simple because the work at hand and the changing interactions around that work are so unpredictable and complex. (1994, 183)

The predictable, linear structure of the workshop allows what happens *inside* the workshop to be very nonlinear. It allows children and their teachers to create an ecosystem that fosters risk taking and creativity so they can go about the very messy business of learning.

Changing Your Classroom Ecosystem: Bringing Your Reality Closer to Your Vision

Debbie Miller begins her book *Teaching with Intention* with this invitation:

> If I were to ask you to close your eyes and envision the perfect classroom scene, what would you see? What would you hear and smell and feel? Think big! If everything were going just the way you'd like it to, what would be happening? What would your kids be doing? How about you? (2008, 10)

This exercise in reflection is an important one and one that we can—and should—practice over and over again as teachers. Take a moment and pause to ask yourself, "How does what I envision match what is happening now?" and "What can I do to draw the two closer together?" Our classroom ecosystems are ever evolving. They are influenced by demands from beyond our control and by our own learning and growth as educators. Most importantly, they are influenced by our children and by regularly asking ourselves, "What can I do to create an environment that fosters energized learning and growth?"

TIPS FOR GETTING STARTED ON CREATING AN ECOSYSTEM FOR GROWTH

- Learn about where your students will typically fall in terms of social, emotional, academic, and physical development.
- Fine-tune your kid watching skills. Think about how you can get to know and teach the whole child, not just his math, reading, and writing profiles. (See Chapter 2 for more on kid watching.)
- Create a list of your nonnegotiables when it comes to teaching and learning. Use that lens to look at your schedule and your curriculum. Use whatever flexibility you have to align them.
- Look carefully at your classroom environment. Ask yourself, "Does this reflect what I value?" and "How are my students represented in this environment?" At the beginning of the year you may want to think of your classroom as a blank canvas—literally and figuratively—ready to be filled by what you and your students create together.
- Find people you can connect with and learn from. Twitter chats, education blogs, and teachers down the hall or across the city can all be sources of encouragement, idea sharing, and support.

Getting to Know Your Learners

Getting to Know Them, Getting to Know All About Them

Teachers live in a world of "start over." From new standards to new students, every school year begins with change. We love the opportunities for reinvention and reinvigoration, new classroom setups, new colleagues, and new possibilities. The day before the first day of school radiates promise and hope. We move tables an inch to the right and then an inch to the left, trying to determine where they work best; we leave the walls open for thinking the students will create; and we pencil in plans. Oftentimes the beginning-of-the-year staff meetings are centered on new policies and curriculum change. Teachers may use open time to study the new math program or prepare materials for the first writing lesson, but we think the most important thing to plan for is how they will get to know their students.

There is no curriculum more powerful than a close and a careful study of your kids. In the overwhelming rush of thinking about where children will need to be, we sometimes forget to find them first where they are. There is nothing more meaningful to a fellow human than to be truly seen and truly heard, and that is what is at the heart of the best instruction. But how do we do it when it feels like the weight of the world is bearing down on us? Deadlines? Standards? Benchmarks? First, take a deep breath; we have more time than we think with our children, and knowing each one of them as a person makes every minute of that time more powerful. As educators, one of our greatest responsibilities and privileges is to get to know each individual child—to learn about each student's passions, fears, habits, and motivations. Knowing a child's reading level is virtually meaningless without knowing the child. Just as dress size tells you nothing about a person's hopes, dreams, fears, and desires, standard assessment measures are limited in their scope. To truly reach and teach every child, we must understand them all as people, to the best of our humble ability.

Making time for this can feel hard, but you can help yourself by seeing each aspect of your day as a chance to learn something more about each child. In our chapter on ecosystems, we talked about using workshop structures and play to allow children space to construct meaning. Use that time to study the unique personality of each child. There is a seemingly endless list of things you can study about your students—their friendships, where they work best in the classroom, what time of day they are most engaged, or how they solve problems, to name a few—but we have found that one of the most important things you can observe is how your students take on the constellation of stances. How and when do they persevere? Why are they more resilient in writing than in math? Are they more empathetic with some children than with others? When you observe your children with these lenses, you can then see the best course of action to make them even more engaged and energized in their learning and in life.

To help you do this, we have gathered together a simple protocol to use. First, be wary of your assumptions. Next, observe your students intentionally and then gather even more information. Finally, look for patterns and use them to guide your interpretation, planning, and teaching.

Suggestions for Learning About Your Kids

In *Choice Words*, Peter Johnston makes a comparison between doctors and educators that speaks to the heart of teaching:

> Becoming a physician requires learning what signs to notice, what to name particular clusters of signs, how to distinguish one drug from another, and how different drugs relate to different patterns of signs. Becoming a

> teacher requires knowing how to tell when learning is going well and when it is not, what children's invented spelling indicates about what they know, what it means when a child does not participate productively, and so forth. . . . This pattern recognition is very powerful. (2004, 11)

Teachers' and physicians' actions are based on a cycle of researching, reflecting, and responding. One February, Christine developed a terrible sore throat and went to see the doctor. Her doctor did not automatically diagnose strep, prescribe penicillin, and send her on her way (despite Christine's extensive online research and self-diagnosis). Even though strep was running rampant around her school and the doctor had diagnosed several patients that week, she did not make an automatic assumption about Christine's case. Instead, she followed her protocol as a physician: she researched, reflected, and responded. Just as physicians cannot and should not rely on assumptions about their patients, teachers cannot and should not rely on assumptions about their students.

However, the longer we teach, the easier it is to fall into saying things such as, "Oh, *Chris*; I've had a kid just like Chris before." Or to peg a child's entire personality on the way she doesn't exhibit persistence but instead abandons her work after five minutes of the first writing workshop. Sometimes these snap judgments happen because we feel like we don't have the time to get to know each child, or sometimes they happen without us even realizing that we're doing it. In her book *How to Stay Sane*, psychoanalyst Philippa Perry cautioned against getting overly comfortable with our quick and simplistic assessments of others: "If we get too set in our ways, we are less able to be touched, moved or enlightened by another and we lose vitality. And we need to allow ourselves to be open to the impact of the other if we are to impact upon them" (2009, 42).

Why are we teachers if not to make an impact on others? This street runs two ways, and we must be open to challenging our own assumptions about people. Such assumptions are dangerous and can prevent us from seeing a child as he really is—capable, curious, and ready to negotiate the complexities of the world in his very own way.

This process is messy and challenging. It cannot be completed in the first week of school and then checked off our ever-expanding to-do list. Rather, it must extend throughout the year and drive our planning, our teaching, and our every interaction with each child. To do this well, we must take on the role of a researcher in our very own classrooms. We don't mean that we should give up teaching and start conducting controlled trials, but rather that we should take on some qualities of researchers. (For some resources on teacher-researchers, see Appendix A.)

To begin to see our children clearly, we must start by seeing our own complex minds as the lenses through which all information passes. We all come into our classrooms and our role as teacher-researchers with prejudices—with a set of ideas that we might not be acutely aware of but that draw our attention and inform our judgment and lead us to make assumptions. These might be assumptions that

STUDYING OUR OWN INTERACTION STYLES LEADS TO BETTER RELATIONSHIPS

Many of our interactions with people exist below our conscious radar. It is only when we stop to reflect that we find the way we relate to people comes with its own set of hidden rules. In *How to Stay Sane*, Perry (2009) articulates three ways that our mind's inner workings can lead us to make assumptions that cause us to "get it wrong" when we interact with other people:

- First, you might project yourself onto the other person, so instead of having an I–you relationship, you have an I–I relationship. In that case, you assume, "She will respond just as I would respond." For example, you might give feedback to students in a certain way because that is how *you* would want to receive it. This is problematic because there is only one you; no matter how many people you meet, no one will think and act exactly the same as you do. The I–you alternative in this scenario is to ask, "What kind of feedback works best for you?"
- Second, you might objectify the other person and have an I–it relationship. "If I phrase it like this, she will think of me like that." Who doesn't long for control? It is, sadly, a fallacy that we can create specific responses in other people. As a classroom teacher, you might fall into this trap when you ask a question that you *think* has an obvious answer and the child responds with something completely unexpected.
- Finally, you might blur the boundaries between the person with you in the present and people you have known before. You can transfer your experience of people from the past onto this person in the present and have an I–ghost relationship. "If I do this, other people always respond like that." In the classroom, you might experience this as thinking, "This strategy always worked for Connor, so it will work for Athena."

Knowing our own minds, and our own complex ways of dealing with others, can help us as people and as teachers learn how to push our own assumptions aside. When we do this, we become open to the impact of others and increase our ability to impact in return.

attract us, distract us, or simply just push our buttons. (For more on how we might make assumptions about our students and others, see the box "Studying Our Own Interaction Styles Leads to Better Relationships").

It is not just what we think we already know that can cause us to assume incorrectly; it is also the myriad of things we might not know about others' experiences and cultures. Philippa Perry cautions against making assumptions about people based on ignorance: "You may act in a caring way towards somebody, but if you have not absorbed the rules of that person's family of origin or culture you can still get it wrong" (2009, 51). Prejudices and assumptions based on ignorance are especially important for us to be aware of as teachers, who—no matter where we teach—work with a diverse group of families and cultures. As you'll see in this chapter's case study about Carlos, if we're not careful, our assumptions have the potential to deeply affect how we understand and interact with a child.

A CLASSROOM CASE STUDY: GETTING TO KNOW CARLOS

It was the Friday after an exhausting first week in kindergarten when Valerie and her assistant teacher, Jenna, sat down to talk. They compared things they had noticed about the children, reflected on who was settling into the routines and classroom, who was taking risks and making friends, and who was giving them pause. As they went through the class list, talking and reflecting, they both sighed for a moment when they came to Carlos. In the one week since school had started, five-year-old Carlos had bitten three students; hid in the closet during choice time; covered his ears and turned his back on every teacher he had encountered, even when he or she just bent down to ask how it was going; and finally announced, "I do not have to leave recess until I am done playing."

Jenna, a grad student finishing her special education degree, was firm in her belief that Carlos thought the rules of school were not for him and suggested using a sticker chart to celebrate when Carlos worked successfully with the community. Valerie, who had been working on her "assume nothing" stance, was not so sure that this was an instance of a child feeling too self-confident or needing a sticker incentive to follow community expectations. Couldn't his bluster also be a sign of something else? She pushed aside her personal feelings of frustration about the behavior and instead suggested they take a week or so to observe closely why and when these incidents occurred.

Like Christine's sore throat, Carlos' behavior was symptomatic of something. But what? Assumptions could exacerbate the issue, and like any doctor, Valerie and Jenna needed more information.

Observe Intentionally

The first thing physicians do when they are trying to make a diagnosis is to observe carefully and intentionally. They look at your throat, your ears, your eyes. They listen to your heart and check your pulse and your breathing. They look for clues, or a particular cluster of signs, as Peter Johnston writes, that will lead to them to the correct diagnosis. Teacher-researchers do the same thing: we don't make assumptions about our students; instead we carefully observe their actions, conversations, affects, and emotions. Then, we reflect on and interpret those findings and use them to plan and guide our every interaction with those children.

As teachers, if we take on this same stance of intentional observation, we can learn what moves will make our interactions with a child especially meaningful and our teaching especially effective. It can seem overwhelming to take on this role as a researcher, so we suggest that you start small.

Observation: Tips to Get Started

- Often it is best to start with a particular question about a child. In Valerie and Jenna's case, they asked, "What precedes Carlos' difficult moments?"
- Find just five or ten minutes to sit down with the intention of kid watching. These minutes could be a part of choice time, math partner work, or even snack time. Make sure your focus can be on noticing and taking notes and doesn't need to be on directly teaching. You'll be surprised how much you can observe in just a few minutes.
- Make yourself as unobtrusive as possible. If your children are sitting at a table, sit at the same level a few feet away. If they are reading in the library, sit down on the floor within earshot. Your goal is to be able to research what is happening, not provide instruction or guidance.
- Make this time sacred. In any class, from kindergarten to fifth grade, a teacher sitting quietly at a table is like an open invitation for children to come up and ask questions and ask for your attention. Just as you would with a reading or writing conference, gently remind your students that your focus is on other students and that you can give them your attention in a few moments.
- Take detailed notes on what you see and hear. Later, you'll use these notes and observations to form theories about your question.
- Most questions about children are not answered in a single setting. Find multiple times throughout a week to gather a collection of observations.

In *Reflecting Children's Lives: A Handbook for Planning Your Child-Centered Curriculum*, Deb Curtis and Margie Carter offer some additional guidelines for observing students (2011, 107–8):

- **Objectivity:** Write down exactly what you hear and see; don't add any interpretation or reflection of the event. Remember: assume nothing. For example, "looks sad" is subjective; "frowning, hands in fists" is objective. What we assume is sadness could be anger, frustration, embarrassment, or something else.
- **Specificity:** Write using as much specific detail as possible—the more detail you have, the easier it will be to later draw conclusions. "Block tower falls" is not as specific as "Block tower falls when C. puts on next block." This specificity will help you identify possible causes and effects later on.
- **Directness:** Include as many direct quotes as you can; some people choose to use an audio recorder to capture conversations more completely.
- **Completeness:** Make your notes as complete as possible. Include the setting, names of the people who are present, and their reactions, tones of voice, facial expressions, body positions, hand gestures, and so on.

CLASSROOM CASE STUDY: GETTING TO KNOW CARLOS

As the week went on, Jenna and Valerie took turns taking notes. Often Valerie would set up an activity like choice time and then start to observe after she had settled the class. Over the course of a week, Jenna and Valerie had collected a clipboard's worth of notes on Carlos that started to show a pattern. Oftentimes the biting, hiding, or ear covering immediately happened after some kind of accident: tagging someone at recess so hard that the classmate fell, tripping in eagerness to get to the block center and knocking down a preexisting tower, lining up with the wrong class. Carlos, like many five-year-olds, was impulsive and active. His body awareness, like that of many five-year-olds, was still developing. It was beginning to seem that typical accidents for five-year-olds were not met with typical reactions from Carlos. He would bite the person who said, "Ow," would hide after his body acted in ways he could not control, and would cover his ears when a teacher bent down to ask him, "What happened?"

Valerie's instincts were starting to look accurate; it was not that Carlos did not want to work with the community, but that he had a difficult time rebounding from accidents. But why?

Over time, observing children will start to feel like second nature to you. Your students will quickly grow accustomed to seeing you a few feet away, clipboard in hand (see Appendix C for a possible kid watching form). You'll find yourself dashing across your classroom for your notebook or scribbling quick notes on a scrap of paper to capture a moment and freeze it in time. You will also find that one question, one wondering, will quickly lead to another. You'll start to hold in your head—and in your notebook—not one question, but several.

In the case of Valerie and Jenna, the more they observed Carlos, the more apparent a pattern became and the more they found themselves *really* starting to see Carlos.

Gather More Information and Develop a Working Theory

Physicians do not rely on observation alone to make a diagnosis. Instead, they use as many sources as they have at their disposal to gather as much information as they possibly can. They ask questions, both to themselves and to their patient; they conduct tests; they consult experts; and they read journals. The more difficult the question is to answer, the more sources of information they seek and use.

The same holds true for us as teachers. While observing children anchors our research, we often must use other methods to gather data and learn about our students. The harder our questions are to answer and the more we find ourselves saying, "Perhaps it's because . . . ," or "I wonder . . . ," the more data we collect. Using additional sources of data helps us see the complexities that lie behind our questions. In *The Art of Classroom Inquiry*, Ruth Shagoury Hubbard and Brenda Miller Power (2003) suggest the following sources for gathering additional information about your students as you try to answer a particular question or wondering:

- **Examine student work and classroom artifacts (59).** Look closely at students' work—anything from formal writing pieces to scraps of paper doodled on at lunch. Date everything and develop a system for organizing student work that works for you.
- **Create audiotape and videotape transcripts (78).** Record conversations between children or the whole class and analyze the data later.
- **Take photographs (84).** Use photographs to complement written observations, to help jog your memory about an observation, or to gather data quickly.

- **Ask questions (63).** When you are asking a child questions, listen actively, take your time, write down key information, and be flexible in your questioning. Ask open-ended, follow-up, and summarizing questions.

As with all observations, the more we know, the more we see. Chapter 3 will help you look for the constellation of stances that make for energized and engaged learning and living, but there are a myriad of other lenses through which you might study children and their artifacts (for more lenses on what to study, see the box "Additional Lenses of Observation and Reflection").

ADDITIONAL LENSES OF OBSERVATION AND REFLECTION

- **Learning Sequences:** For each academic domain (math, reading, writing, spelling) there is a corresponding developmental sequence (see Appendix A for a list of resources). Although the sequences are not entirely linear for all children, knowing and understanding the sequences—and where your children are along those sequences—is critical to effective teaching and learning.
- **Physical Development:** The physical development of children can seem rather straightforward: children grow and gain more skills. But in reality, it's full of nuances. As a teacher you'll want to use this lens to study your children's fine motor skills (the small, precise movements, such as connecting Legos and writing with a pencil) and gross motor skills (the larger movements, such as running and balancing on a beam).
- **Language Development:** When studying your students' language development, you'll want to notice both their expressive and their receptive language. Expressive language skills address how children communicate with language and include their speech, sentence formation, and command of norms. Receptive language skills address how children take in and understand language, including how they follow directions and understand stories.
- **Social and Emotional Growth:** The importance of social and emotional growth cannot be underscored enough and is the foundation for much of this book. In addition to a child's growth as an individual, you'll want to study how she develops friendships, interacts with adults, and views and interacts with the world at large.

As you collect data, you'll begin to weave it into a theory or a story about that student. The more data you collect, the more vivid your theory will become.

TIPS FOR DEVELOPING A WORKING THEORY

Here are some suggestions from *The Art of Classroom Inquiry* (Hubbard and Power 2003).

- Start developing a theory when you start collecting information. Jot a theory on a sticky note or on the side of your notebook.
- Set aside time to sit down and reread your notes.
- Think about what you notice. Are there any patterns that seem to be developing? You may want to go back through your notes and code bits of information.
- Triangulate your theory with multiple sources. Does your theory hold true when you analyze student work or photographs or speak with another educator?
- Test your theory by gathering more information.
- Trust that your brain will be working on this theory, even when you are not aware of it. Also trust those aha moments when your theory is confirmed or revised.

Compiling and studying this information is best done in the company of someone who can help you hear your own prejudices or offer alternative ways of thinking. You will not always be right, but even the wrong step can lead you toward the right one.

Treat the Cause, Not Just the Symptoms

Once a physician has gathered all of the information she needs, she uses that data, and her best judgment, to make a diagnosis and prescribe a course of treatment. Christine's doctor did not treat just the symptoms of her illness (her fever, her sore throat, her headache) but also the cause (the big reveal: it was strep all along!). Ibuprofen, rest, and fluids might have treated the symptoms for some time but would not have addressed the real reason that she was sick.

Teacher-researchers must do the same thing. Once we have gathered all of the information we could about a student, a situation, or a particular question, we interpret that data and use it to address what is at the root of a student's actions. We then think, "How can I help a student who is more resilient in writing than in math transfer that habit?" or "Would flexibility help this student when he feels trapped and stuck?" In *The Art of Classroom Inquiry*, Hubbard and Power write, "Data analysis is a way of seeing and then seeing again. It is the process of bringing order, structure, and meaning to the data, to discover what is underneath the surface of the classroom" (2003, 88).

CLASSROOM CASE STUDY: GETTING TO KNOW CARLOS

Jenna and Valerie sat down and developed a bit of a working theory about Carlos after a week of observation of Carlos at play: Carlos bites, hides, and covers his ears (A kind of hiding? they wondered) after accidents occurred. Carlos would also demonstrate a kind of bravado after accidents occurred, saying, "I don't care," or "This is boring." When they considered all these observations together, it started to seem like Carlos did not know how to process his feelings when something happened that made himself or others upset. His habit of hiding suggested that he might be fearful of what he would hear or see after an accident, and when a child voiced displeasure, he seemed to cope with his own feelings by acting in aggressive ways.

Valerie sat next to Carlos one day to see if he could shed any light on this behavior, knowing that he was just five and this would possibly go nowhere. As Carlos built with Legos, Valerie asked: "Do you know what an accident is?" Carlos continued to snap bricks together and did not answer. Valerie put a hand on Carlos' back and tried another attempt. "Cool Lego structure," she said. "What are you making?"

Carlos continued to work but answered this time. "The *Millennium Falcon*."

Valerie smiled at this opening. "Aaah, so you are a *Star Wars* expert?" she asked.

"Actually, I am really Luke Skywalker," he said. "I am making this for my friend Han Solo."

"Aaah," Valerie said, peering intently at the ship. "You have lots of little details in here, huh?" Carlos nodded as he snapped another piece in place, and Valerie continued. "You know, it takes a long time to be a Jedi. You have to go through lots of training, and sometimes you aren't very good at it, you know, like when Luke was learning to use the force with Yoda."

Carlos stopped and looked at Valerie for the first time. "I saw that movie," he said.

"Great! Then you know what I am talking about." Valerie smiled encouragingly. "You know how Luke had such a hard time raising the ship out of the swamp, and he even dropped Yoda that time?" Carlos nodded. "Those were accidents, like sometimes when you try something new or hard and you mess up—that's an accident."

Carlos nodded. "Yeah, yeah, and you know, accidents are bad. Bad people can do accidents and hurt people."

Valerie felt a pang as she heard the phrase "bad people" and asked, "What do you mean?"

Carlos shrugged.

Valerie smiled and rubbed his back. "Well, sometimes accidents can *feel* bad, but that doesn't mean that they are bad or that bad people do them. Like Luke isn't bad; it was just a kind of thing that happened when he was trying to learn something. Mistakes and accidents can help you more than hurt you."

Carlos looked at Valerie for a moment and went back to snapping together Legos. It wasn't much, but Valerie thought it was a start, to be picked back up later. Now, what to do with this information?

This process of reseeing our classroom allows us to truly get to know our students and plan exactly which lessons, interactions, or opportunities would best nurture their growth.

CLASSROOM CASE STUDY: GETTING TO KNOW CARLOS

Valerie and Jenna then fixed everything. The end.

No, not really, but that is how these case studies can feel sometimes when we read them at home while thinking of our own challenging students. The truth of the matter is that at recess the same day, Carlos hid in the bathroom when he was reminded of the school rule that slides are for going down only. However, Jenna and Valerie had connected with Carlos through this process so that they had the ability to see his behavior as that of a little boy who struggled with not being perfect. He truly feared what a mistake said about him, so Jenna and Valerie began a slow and steady process of teaching him that a mistake means nothing about who you are as a person and what you can do. They began first by looking him in the eye, with a reassuring hand on his shoulder, and saying, "You are really brave for trying that. It did not go exactly how you wanted, huh? You know we love you a lot, right?" They suspected what Carlos might want was reassurance that a mistake changed nothing about him or their feelings about him, and so they made sure to let him know that as often as possible. The first time Valerie tried it, when Carlos was covering his ears and yelling that he would not listen, he burst into tears when she got to "I love you" and went in for a hug from her.

A sticker chart for working with the community, though possibly addressing his behavior in the short term, would do nothing for the root cause of Carlos' actions, which were motivated by fear and insecurity. To be truly honest, Valerie admitted that Carlos was a challenging student and that she sometimes had to take a deep breath and remind herself that when he covered his ears or said, "I don't care," he was just protecting himself. Helping him feel secure when he made mistakes had to be paired with swapping out his traditional coping mechanisms (hiding or biting) with more productive and powerful ones (taking some space and then fixing what needed to be fixed).

More than stickers, Carlos needed resilience and optimism, and through the course of a year, by using the strategies in this book, Carlos began to develop them. Compliance can be a long way from agency and a healthy mindset. We must always ask ourselves, as Jenna and Valerie did, not "What do I need from this child?" but "What does this child need from me to be healthy, successful, and happy?"

The Value of Connections

Through the case study about Carlos we have seen Valerie and Jenna strive to better understand one student through careful and close observation, yet as they did this, they also were working to get to know every student. Sometimes it can feel like a child like Carlos constitutes 90 percent of the day, and some children will need more intense and thoughtful observation, as he did. However, we must make time to discover the unique inner world of every child, whether the child is quiet, loud, shy, or gregarious. Through close study, Valerie began to realize she had a few students that were like Carlos in their views on accidents and mistakes, and others who had less than positive mindsets on trying new things or on working with others. If she and Jenna hadn't taken the time to kid watch, some of these issues might have slipped under the radar and been categorized as shyness or laziness.

Various studies have found a direct positive correlation between the warmth of the relationships between students and their teachers and the academic success of students (Hattie and Yates 2013, 17). Yet it can feel like schools prioritize everything over the slow and careful process of connecting with each and every child. Therefore, it is up to us, the teachers, to make time and space for forming connections. This is not an either-or scenario; it is a *while* scenario. It is not *teach writing or get to know the kids*; it's *while teaching writing, get to know the kids*. To do this well, we must take the step to remove ourselves and our assumptions from the slate, so that we can truly observe and connect with our students.

Making connections goes beyond just knowing students' passions, though that is critically important; it also involves getting to know their styles of learning, their motivations, their fears, and their mindsets. There are numerous books that will teach you how to connect to various learning styles but few that can help you learn how to teach into positive stances of being in the world. What really helps children become energized and engaged learners? Active and empathic individuals? People who are joyful and resilient in the face of challenge? A combination of things, but only through carefully studying your students and making meaningful connections will you be able to create a lasting positive impact. The following chapter outlines the constellation of stances we found most helpful to observe for in our students and in ourselves.

Knowledge Is Power: Teaching Children the Constellation of Stances

Have you ever had this happen to you: you start thinking about something—maybe a new hairstyle or a certain color car you might want to buy—and then, all of a sudden, you start to notice that thing more and more often? One moment you might be contemplating getting bangs and the next you find yourself running into women with bangs everywhere you look. Then you start to analyze each and every one of their hairstyles. By focusing our attention on something specific, we gain an increased sense of awareness of its presence in our world and we start to think about it more critically. It's as if we put on a special pair of glasses and we start to see the world through a new set of lenses. It seems simple enough but, in reality, it can be powerful. This new lens can serve as a call to action for things we notice about our world (the litter on our block, acts of injustice in our community) as well as a call to reflection for things we notice about ourselves (our habits, our decisions, and our very outlook on life).

When Christine was running almost daily while training for a race, she started to notice a strange pattern. On days when life got busy and she had to skip her run, she would see runners everywhere she went—on the way to work, outside the window of her classroom, zipping around the neighborhood. It's as if the runners were taunting her, "We fit it in! Why can't you?" No matter the day of the week, or the time of year, or the weather, on the days she skipped running, there seemed to be runners everywhere. There was not a dramatic increase in the number of runners on those days, just one in Christine's awareness of them. All day her focus shifted back to the fact that she was skipping a day of running and, by doing so, she gained a level of consciousness that she didn't have on days when she focused on her own run instead. More often than not, after noticing just how many people got out to run, she would slip into her running shoes at the very end of the day and squeeze in a quick run. By raising her awareness, she not only changed her observations but also her behavior.

What we choose to focus our attention on—the good, the bad, the ugly, or the beautiful—can dramatically change our behavior and interactions with the world. For our students, what we guide their awareness to can have a powerful effect on their lives. What lenses will be the most powerful for them to see themselves, and the world, through?

Harnessing the Power of Awareness

Just as gaining awareness of runners or bangs can change our day-to-day decisions, gaining awareness of how we view ourselves and the process of learning and thinking can change how we react to new challenges and life's inevitable setbacks. In *Mindset: The New Psychology of Success*, Carol Dweck articulates the power of shifting our awareness: "Just by knowing about the two mindsets," she writes, "you can start thinking and reacting in new ways" (2007, 46). (See the introduction for more on Dweck's mindset work.) The knowledge of the fixed and growth mindsets alone is enough to stop people in their tracks and change both their thinking and their actions.

Or put another way, psychologist Martin E. P. Seligman writes in *Learned Optimism*, "Our thoughts are not merely reactions to events; they change what ensues" (2006, 7). The more aware we are of our thinking, Seligman argues, the more control we have over our actions. For example, Kristi's friend once snapped during a conversation, "Stop trying to *fix* everything; just listen!" Until that moment, Kristi hadn't even realized that she was doing that. Now, knowing that her tendency is to swoop in and try to solve every problem, she tries to bite her tongue when she wants to say, "Well have you tried . . . ?" Awareness illuminates the difference between choice and inevitability. We always have a choice in our own thinking and behavior. As teachers, we can harness this power of awareness, choice, and action, and use it as a natural first step in our work to foster engaged and energized learners.

Defining the Stances of Engaged and Energized Learners

Though the following list of stances is by no means exhaustive, they are the habits of mind that came up again and again in the research we read (for more on our research, see the list of works cited). For the children we teach, by intentionally and explicitly introducing this constellation of stances—optimism, flexibility, persistence, resilience, and empathy—we are laying the foundation for the work to come on self-talk, storytelling, goal setting, and reflection. Our goal is not for students to use each of these stances in isolation; instead we see these stances as a tool kit that students can use when faced with a challenge, oftentimes in coordination. We have found, however, that it is helpful to teach the stances one by one and then to notice, as a class, when and how the stances weave and work together. (See the chart "The Constellation of Stances and Their Definitions" later in this chapter for a quick guide.)

Optimism

Optimism is feeling hopeful that risks are worth taking and that problems will work their way out. Here's a beginning definition to use with children: *When you do something new, you think, "I can try," and give it your best shot because that's how you grow.*

The glass is half full; every cloud has a silver lining; if life has given you lemons, you might as well make lemonade. You know and have heard these expressions countless times. But the truth is that optimism is actually very powerful.

Imagine this scenario: You teach about adding dialogue to a narrative only to have the lesson flop miserably (and we know they do sometimes). Students leave the lesson confused, and you start conferring with students despite a nagging sense of failure. That afternoon after school, when you jot down notes for tomorrow's lessons, you have two choices: you can choose optimism or you can choose pessimism.

According to Martin Seligman in *Learned Optimism*,

> the defining characteristic of pessimists is that they tend to believe bad events will last a long time, will undermine everything they do and are their own fault. The optimists, who are confronted with the same hard

> knocks in the world, think about misfortune in the opposite way. They tend to believe defeat is just a temporary setback, that its causes are confined to this one case. The optimists believe that defeat is not their fault: Circumstances, bad luck, or other people brought it about. Such people are unfazed by defeat. Confronted by a bad situation, they perceive it as a challenge and try harder. (2006, 5)

If you face your lesson setback with pessimism, you're likely to think things such as, "I'm such a bad writing teacher," or "I really messed up and now my students will always be confused about adding dialogue." Or you might even blame others for your own feelings of failure: "Dialogue is too hard for kids." It's easy to see how this kind of pessimism spirals into helplessness and unproductivity.

If you face your setback with optimism, you'll likely reflect on just why the lesson didn't work out and plan a new way to teach the lesson. You'll see the setback as temporary and you will accept it as a challenge that you can work through and ultimately overcome with all you know as a teacher. You will find learning in your struggle and use it to become better.

Young children are, on the whole, very optimistic. When children are young, many take risks almost without a second thought: jumping off rocks into puddles, playing experimentally with words and sounds, and seeing just what will happen if they pull that worm up from the soil. Seligman writes that for young children, "bad events just happen along, melt away quickly and are someone else's fault" (2006, 126). As children grow up, they often become more wary of taking risks and more helpless in the face of defeat. Children can lose their sense of optimism in several ways: by seeing adults model pessimism, by hearing critical feedback after a failure, and by experiencing early loss or trauma (Seligman 2006, 133). They can grow timid and afraid to take on challenging tasks, happier to just coast along where they are comfortable and maintain a high level of success. As teachers, many of us know these children well. In many school settings they look like the ideal child—well behaved, quiet, and on task. However, these students shrink away when faced with a challenge and are rarely truly energized about their learning.

The good news is that optimism can be taught and that, as Seligman writes, "when the skills of optimism are learned early, they become fundamental" (253). When we teach children in our classrooms to practice optimism, we teach them to launch themselves into difficult tasks with the belief that even if they fail, they can learn and grow and that any problems they face will work themselves out one way or another. We teach them to hold on to that sense of curiosity and wonder from their earliest years and to continue asking, "What if?" unafraid of what the answer might be.

Flexibility

Being flexible means seeing and trying many possible actions within a task. A beginning definition to use with children is: *When one thing doesn't work, you try a different way.*

Try to remember the last time you were lost. What did you do? Did you check the map on your phone? Refer back to the directions? Stop and ask for help? Retrace your route? Chances are, you thought carefully about several of these options and then used the one that you thought would be the most successful. Now, what if you decided to check the map on your phone and you found you were out of cell phone range? You'd most likely use this new information to rethink the problem and choose an alternate solution—maybe now it would be time to pull into a gas station and ask for directions. Whatever the solution, the important thing is that you were flexible. You didn't merely drive around in circles, hoping that your destination would magically appear in front of you.

This flexibility in thinking is critical to solving problems. In *Discovering and Exploring Habits of Mind*, Arthur Costa and Bena Kallick describe flexible people: "They have the capacity to change their minds as they receive additional data. They engage in multiple and simultaneous outcomes and activities, and they draw upon a repertoire of problem-solving strategies" (2000, 25). Thinking flexibly requires you to consider all of the possible approaches to a problem, to assess which will be the most helpful, and to employ it. Thinking flexibly also requires you to reassess the problem and your actions every time it changes or you receive more information.

Costa and Kallick go on to suggest that flexibility includes being able to see a problem from one's own perspective (or what Jean Piaget called egocentrism), another's perspective (allocentrism), a bird's-eye view (macrocentrism), and a worm's-eye view (microcentrism) (2000, 26). By quickly shifting between these perspectives, flexible thinkers can "approach a problem from a new angle, using a novel approach" (22) what Edward de Bono called "lateral thinking." It is this lateral thinking that allows us to know if finding our way will simply mean taking the next left or changing routes entirely.

Flexibility, for the children in our classrooms, means seeing all of the possible actions they could take in a given scenario. It means that when one strategy to subtract three-digit numbers doesn't work, they can switch to another. It means knowing when a book is too challenging for them and choosing something just right. It means when they have a problem with a friend, they have a menu of options to stand up for themselves or repair the relationship. But in the long term, flexibility will also allow these children, and the adults they will become, to see large, complex problems and find ways to tackle them efficiently and creatively.

Resilience

Resilience is the ability to bounce back and recover from setbacks or failures. Here's a beginning definition to use with children: *When you have trouble, you bounce back and try again.*

In their book *Building Resilience in Children and Teens*, Kenneth Ginsburg and Martha Jablow (2011) use a beach ball metaphor to illustrate resilience: Imagine a ball floating on the ocean, they suggest. No matter how far down you push it, it will always come back to the surface.

Our own resiliency is tested and measured every day. How quickly do we recover when we lock ourselves out of the house? Or burn dinner? Or get lost? Do we rebound within a few moments, solve the problem, and move on? Or do we linger with the issue and let it define our day or even our week? Of course, how resilient we are is directly affected by the nature and scope of the situation.

Resilience is important in our day-to-day lives, but it is essential to learning. Resilience is what allows one to be persistent. It is the ability to stand up after a fall, try again after a mistake, and love again after heartbreak. It is the ability to come back into yourself and try again. The tried-and-true bike-riding analogy fits perfectly here: when you're learning to ride a bike you will fall, you will probably get scraped up a bit, and you might even have some scary close calls. But what is most important is that you get back on the bike and keep trying. You do not melt into a puddle of frustration and never ride again; you bounce back and get back on the bike again and again. Without resilience when learning something new, learning becomes next to impossible.

Ginsburg and Jablow suggest, "Some children seem naturally graced with an ability to recover from obstacles, while others need extra support" (2011, 4). As teachers, we see this every day, even if we haven't named it as resilience until now. We see some students who are buoyed quickly back to the surface and others who seem to spiral farther and farther downward with every setback. While giving up on the task at hand meets students' immediate need for escape, there are longer-term consequences at stake (Ginsburg and Jablow 2011, 14). Students who do not develop their resilience can instead develop an aversion to taking risks. Edwin Catmull, the CEO of Pixar, and his coauthor, Amy Wallace, warn against this aversion to failure: "If you aren't experiencing failure, then you are making a far worse mistake: You are being driven by the desire to avoid it" (2014, 109).

Resilience can be learned and can be developed in ourselves and in the children we teach. By creating an environment where children feel comfortable with taking just-right risks and failing (see the section "Understanding Development in Order to Create Just-Right Risks" in Chapter 1 for more information on setting up just-right challenges), we are allowing them to experience the predictable pattern of attempting, running into difficulty, and resetting. This is not to say that the difficult moments won't feel bad—of course they will—but rather that those bad feelings can be overcome and do not define their personhood. The more often they feel that bounce-back, the more habitual it will become.

Persistence

Sticking with something even when it is challenging requires persistence. You might describe it for children this way: *Having persistence means you try and try again even when it feels hard.*

Persistence, sometimes used in the same breath as grit, is one of the more debated stances in the research we have read. To understand why, it is useful to consider persistence in our own day-to-day experiences. Relationships are the perfect lens to think critically about the pros and cons of persistence.

Persistence in relationships can be an unhealthy approach; imagine the time you worked and worked at a relationship that just seemed to go nowhere. Maybe the scenario was calling and calling someone long after he or she ceased calling you back. Maybe the scenario was believing that if you just kept up your end of the bargain, the other person would change and start treating you differently. Either way, persistence in such cases is more harmful than helpful. Doggedness in the face of clear callousness, disregard, or unrealistic expectations is damaging to a degree beyond measure. There are some things you should just let go.

Yet persistence can also save and strengthen relationships. When a beloved friend goes through a challenging time and seems to disappear, it is persistence on your end, through calls, visits, and check-ins, that ensures you will still have a friendship in the future. Even great marriages can have tough spots, but a desire to try and try to resolve the issues can lead to stronger and more powerful connections. As Ernest Hemingway said in *A Farewell to Arms* "the world breaks every one and afterward many are strong at the broken places" (1957, 249).

To persist or not to persist? That is the question. The answer: sometimes. We refer to these stances as tools; sometimes you need a hammer and other times you need a screwdriver. We value reflection (see Chapters 11 and 12) for this purpose: so we can fine-tune our personal understandings of when and why each stance helps (or hurts) our growth.

Grit is a term that we've been seeing more and more in education circles. Angela Duckworth, a professor of psychology at the University of Pennsylvania, has defined grit as "staying with one path. Grit is choosing to show up and again" (Lewis 2014, 182). Anders Ericsson defines this type of practice as "deliberate practice." By trying something over and over again—even in the face of setbacks—students can harness their grit to propel their growth.

On the other hand, there are times when persistence or grit is no longer helpful to growth. In an article published in the *Washington Post*, education author and lecturer Alfie Kohn defined these times as "non-productive persistence" (2014). He wrote,

> [Gritty people] try, try again, though the result may be either unremitting failure or "a costly or inefficient success that could have been easily surpassed by alternative courses of action," as Dean McFarlin and his colleagues put it in the *Journal of Personality* [1984]. Even if you don't crash and burn by staying the course, you may not fare nearly as well as if you had stopped, reassessed and tried something else.

But what if having a greater purpose for your work actually made you grittier when you needed to be? People who change the world do so in part because they have grit. In a recent study by David Yeager of the University of Texas at Austin and others, the researchers found that teenagers who wanted to make a positive impact on their community or society found their schoolwork to be more meaningful: "Initial promising results suggest the psychology strategy could encourage pupils to plug away at homework or learning tasks that are challenging or tedious, yet necessary to getting an education that'll help them reach their greater life goals" (Chen 2014). When students see the link between the task at hand and their potential future impact on their community or society, Yeager reports, their "grittiness" actually increases. Daniel Pink has written extensively on the link between purpose and drive; for more on motivation and the importance of purpose, including Pink's thoughts on the subject, see Chapters 9 and 10.

As teachers, we must teach children when to use persistence to catapult them up and over a learning hurdle and when that tenaciousness is what it will take to be successful. However, for persistence to be an effective tool, it must be coupled with the other stances in the constellation.

Empathy

Empathy is the ability to feel how another person is feeling and imagine what it would be like to be in another's position. A beginning definition to use with children is *You have empathy when you feel someone's feelings in your own heart.*

Do you have a friend, or a partner, whom you go to in times of need? A person who seems to radiate warmth and good intention? A person who *understands* you and what you are feeling? Now also imagine the opposite. Do you know someone who is almost clinical in his or her treatment of others, seemingly cold and detached, incapable of seeing your point of view? One of these two people has high levels of what we call empathy.

Empathy, in the words of Daniel Pink in *A Whole New Mind*, "is the ability to stand in others' shoes, to see with their eyes, and to feel with their hearts" (2005, 159). This may seem like a mushy, feel-good idea with no inherent value in learning and leading, but in his foreword to *Roots of Empathy*, Daniel Siegel writes, "Children who develop social and emotional competence are happier, have more rewarding relationships with their peers, are resilient in the face of stress, and even perform better academically" (Gordon 2005, xiv). From doctors, to lawyers, to leaders, Daniel Pink (2005) has found that empathetic individuals deliver better care, make better decisions, and experience greater joy. There is a clear logic to this outcome: the better you understand people, the better you can help them. Beyond this added value, it is worth being empathetic just for the sake of it.

As teachers, we must stay cognizant of the future world we are contributing to. Who do we want in the world? What do we want to foster in our students? Empathy is first and foremost about connecting to and understanding others. All the other stances are meaningless if we fail to value and teach empathy. Empathy provides a system of checks and balances for all other thinking. Is persistence in this goal harmful to myself or others? Can I best support this community through optimism or through flexibility? A world where people exhibit persistence, flexibility, and resilience at the expense of the quality of others' lives is a dark future indeed.

Empathetic children will fight for social justice, equality, and fairness in the classroom, just as we hope they will one day do in the world. Empathy, like every other stance we mention, can be taught starting first, like all the stances, with awareness.

Introducing the Stances: Guided Inquiry and Concept Construction

Let's turn now to introducing this constellation of stances to children. With each stance you introduce, you'll be providing them with a new lens through which they can see the world and themselves. These are exciting moments. Your students will start to see challenges, setbacks, and their own learning in an entirely new light. They will likely feel a greater sense of agency and control over their growth, and the

The Constellation of Stances and Their Definitions

Stance	Memorable Symbol	Definition	Beginning Definition for Students
Optimism		Feeling hopeful that risks are worth taking and that problems will work themselves out.	*When you do something new, you think, "I can try," and give it your best shot because that's how you grow.*
Persistence		Sticking with something even when it is challenging.	*Having persistence means you try and try again even when it feels hard.*
Flexibility		Seeing and trying many possible actions within a task.	*When one thing doesn't work, you try a different way.*
Resilience		Bouncing back and recovering from setbacks or failures.	*When you have trouble, you bounce back and try again.*
Empathy		Feeling how another person is feeling and imagining what it would be like to be in another's position.	*You have empathy when you feel someone's feelings in your own heart.*

class community will be energized as each stance is introduced. Before long, you will hear your students use these lenses throughout their day. You might hear "You were really optimistic when you tried that big slide on the playground even though you'd never done it before" or "I was trying to be flexible when I tried another way to start my personal narrative."

The key to all of this work, however, rests in how the stances are introduced and to what degree students can take ownership of the concepts. To that end, we recommend a balance between guided inquiry and explicit concept instruction. Inquiry is at the heart of constructivism and, therefore, at the heart of our teaching. According to Jean Piaget, learning occurs as you build new knowledge either by transforming or replacing (constructing) existing knowledge. Vygotsky theorized that our learning is based on *social* construction through shared practices and interactions with others. Inquiry provides the perfect opportunity for the shared construction of new learning.

As you will see in the following example from a kindergarten classroom, Malini introduced the stance of empathy to her class by studying a text, in this case a book, and by explicitly teaching the children about the concept.

He Feels Like She Feels—Exploring Empathy: Window into Kindergarten

Welcome to Malini's kindergarten classroom. Amid the blocks and the tables, there are signs that this is not your average kindergarten room. On a wall toward the back of the classroom is a chart that says "Brains Can Grow" (see Figure 3.1). This class has learned that brains, like bodies, grow and that we can do things, like be persistent, to grow our brains. (See Chapter 1 to learn more about setting up a classroom designed to honor growth.)

It is 12:30 p.m. on a Tuesday in mid-September. Lunch has ended and recess has drained some of the wiggles from this group of four- and five-year-olds. The sun is slanting in through the windows on a rainbow-colored rug, the windows are cracked, and the sounds of the city are leaking in, along with a warm breeze. Twenty-four bodies are in various positions of rapt attention as their teacher, Malini, rereads (for the third time this year!) the last few pages of *Leonardo the Terrible Monster*, by Mo Willems (2005), already a class favorite.

- Deeper meaning can often be found on rereads, and children love hearing books again and again.
- Simple texts with powerful pictures can prompt meaningful, and universally accessible, conversations.
- Engagement is not obedience; focused attention is more important than still bodies.

Leonardo has just made a critical decision in the text: instead of pursuing his own dream of becoming a terrible monster, he has decided to become a friend. The pages that precede this moment show Leonardo attempting to scare a very sad boy named Sam, and Sam bursting into tears before launching into a litany of the ways his life is terrible. Malini has frozen here and pauses, leaning forward on her knees in her spot at the front of the rug. "You know, this confused me last time, and it *still* does," she says, with exasperation creeping into her tone. "Why would Leonardo stop wanting to be a monster?!" Malini raises her hands to the ceiling in mock mystification as the voices start piling up.

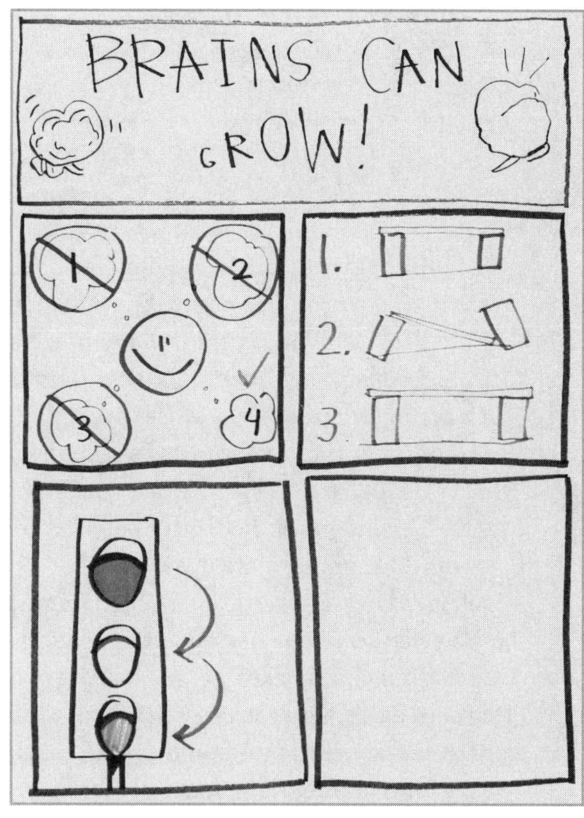

FIGURE 3.1 "Brains Can Grow" Chart

- "Because monsters are bad!"
- "You have to be a friend!"
- "He is a friend!"
- "He's funny!"
- "I have this book!"

This being September of kindergarten, Malini knows to let children say what they need to say for a few moments before gathering their attention again. She flips back to the page before, beautifully illustrated by Mo Willems, where Leonardo and Sam stare at each other with equally horrified expressions. "I want to go back here," Malini says, "because this is what changed his mind. I want to look closer!"

- Sitting low to the ground, or even on the floor, helps establish that the teacher is one of the members of the community and can facilitate a tone of cooperation.
- Implicit in this read-aloud is powerful reading work: rereading a page, stopping when confused, thinking, and talking out confusion.
- For young children, look for picture books with illustrations that engage readers.

Malini holds the book, angling her head one way and then another, asking, "What is going on on this page? Why did Leonardo make such a big change?"

The chorus of voices begins immediately, mostly naming the character actions, faces, and feelings because this is what the students talked about on previous reads. "He is crying! He is sad!" the voices say.

Malini uses these comments to help the children see a connection on the page. "Wait . . . wait. He feels sad? He is crying? Who is crying? Whose face is sad?" As she says this, Malini moves her finger between the two characters, who happen to both be crying and looking quite upset.

"Look! His face [*gesturing to Leonardo*] looks like his face [*gesturing to Sam*]," Jamila yells, launching herself out of her seated position to touch the book.

Malini looks shocked at this discovery and looks to the rest of the children. "Do you see this—do you see what Jamila sees? Do they look the same?" Everyone nods. A few small friends stand to also touch the book, and Malini nods for them to wait for a minute. "The last time we read this," she says, "we thought Sam was sad because he had such a bad day, and now it seems like Leonardo feels sad, too, maybe because Sam is sad?" Heads nod and voices confirm this theory Malini has just offered.

Malini pauses and then says, "So it's like he [*gesturing to Leonardo*] is feeling his feelings [*gesturing to Sam*]? He is feeling sad because Sam is sad?"

"Yeah, yeah, yeah," Boroka shouts. She stands, eager to say what she has just realized. "Leonardo is sad because Sam is sad, like Leonardo's heart is sad. They are sad together!" This last point is punctuated by a flick of the wrist and an open palm, facing upward, and the children around her nod.

- Tackle tricky topics on a reread so the general understanding is already out of the way.
- Gestures often direct the eye; the moment of realization in Malini's classroom is orchestrated by the teacher's nonverbal cueing as she points to the faces.
- Plan to use a book, and a page, that can spark the discussion you want to have, but let students lead you. (See Appendix E for book and video ideas.)

- Though we offer possible starting language for definitions, the best ones will be co-constructed with your students.
- When working with small children, don't underestimate how much repetition will lead to clarity. Though the children seem to be restating, they are actually realizing.

"Wait a minute, wait a minute—has that ever happened to you? Have you ever felt someone else's feelings in your heart, like Boroka said? Like Leonardo here? Turn and tell your neighbor," Malini asks the children. Turn-and-talk is not a flawlessly executed routine yet, so Malini spends a few seconds making sure everyone is actually turned to someone, and she catches only a snippet of what Finn is telling a neighbor (see Figure 3.2).

FIGURE 3.2 Students Turn and Talk

"One time, one time, I saw a girl's ice cream fall on the ground and I felt so sad."

Malini cuts in to repeat the definition they have just constructed. "So, Finn, it was like you felt her feelings in your heart? Like you weren't sad, but you felt her sadness?" Finn nods and Malini offers a whispered, "Whoa."

- Some of the stories the children tell will be fantasies, and it is still OK to treat them as truth; we can pretend ourselves into the people we wish to become. (See also Chapters 7 and 8, on storytelling.)
- Empathy is similar to, but not the same as, sympathy; however, the nuances do not need to be teased out at this moment.
- Move quickly; this is just the beginning of a long journey.

After gathering the attention of the children quickly, Malini recounts the story of Finn and the girl that dropped her ice cream. "Friends," she says, "when you feel someone's feelings in your own heart, there is a big grown-up word that goes with it: *empathy*." Malini writes the word out, quickly, while saying it one more time (see Figure 3.3). Then she asks, "Can we try that word out in our mouths? Let's say it! Empathy! Empathy is when you feel someone's feelings in your own heart, like Finn felt for the girl with the ice cream, or Leonardo did for Sam."

FIGURE 3.3 The Word *Empathy* and an Illustration

- Seeing, saying, and hearing the word activate different areas of the brain and make it more memorable.
- Use a visual, from the book or from a child's story, to illustrate the meaning of the word.
- Speed is more essential than quality, so consider this beginning chart temporary.

Malini notices the wiggles on the rug are increasing after the fifteen minutes this has taken, so she takes the children through a quick calming breath and wraps up. "Friends, we are going to keep our eyes open for when we see empathy or feel empathy in this classroom and in the whole world! We will have a special way and a special place to celebrate each time we grow our hearts and our brains!"

- For more information on the ways empathy is celebrated and kept alive, see the "Reflecting on and Maintaining Growth" section at the end of Chapter 4.

Moving from Idea to Action

By introducing the idea of empathy to her class, Malini has provided a new and highly valuable lens for her kindergartners. In the coming weeks, these four- and five-year-olds will see examples of empathy emerge in every part of their world:

their play, their stories, their homes, and their learning. They'll return to this idea of empathy again and again as a class, celebrating every small act of kindness. When the moment seems right and when her class is ready, Malini will add another stance to her class' tool kit. The following chapter offers a step-by-step guide to introducing the constellation of stances.

Using Guided Inquiry to Teach the Stances

There is no set order for introducing the stances. Just as you choose just-right books or math tasks or instruction for your students, you can choose the just-right order of introduction for your class. Perhaps you teach third grade and after having seen your students try and give up almost immediately, you think your class would benefit by beginning with persistence. Maybe you teach fifth grade and you think the lens of empathy will set the perfect tone at the start of the year. Or, if you teach kindergarten, you might start by teaching optimism, tapping into the inherently playful nature of risk taking.

You will find that once you introduce one stance, it will lead naturally to another stance. Once students get in the habit of "trying and trying again," they might be primed to learn to think flexibly when they come to a roadblock. Or perhaps after students learn to think optimistically, saying, "I can try!" they will need to be introduced to the concept of resilience and practice bouncing back when taking a risk doesn't quite work out. As you introduce each new stance, your students will begin to see their own agency and the powerful role they play in their own learning.

In Your Own Classroom

In a traditional classroom cycle of inquiry, students and teachers launch an inquiry with a question, research that question, interpret their findings, and reflect. (For more on teachers as researchers, see Appendix A.) In *Action, Talk, Text: Learning and Teaching Through Inquiry*, Gordon Wells (2001) describes this cycle as a spiral of knowledge building. Experiences lead to new information, knowledge building, and understanding.

Inquiry can be woven into all areas of your curriculum: reading, writing, science, and social studies. Inquiry can be open-ended and student directed, or it can be guided by the teacher. As we saw in Malini's kindergarten classroom, a guided inquiry provides an opportunity to balance social construction of new learning (in that case, about empathy) with clear, direct instruction about the concept. We recommend the following cycle to introduce each stance:

1. Study a text as a whole class.
2. Discover the concept.
3. Name the concept.
4. Reflect on and generalize the concept.

Study a Text

Your first step, as a class, is to carefully study a text and, through that study, discover one of the five stances of engaged and energized learners. There is a nearly inexhaustible list of texts that you could use to teach each stance. (We've listed some of our favorite resources in Appendix E.) In fact, we've found that many books could be used to teach multiple stances. The lovely picture book *Everyone Can Learn to Ride a Bicycle*, by Chris Rashcka (2013), could be used to teach optimism, persistence, or resilience. Your choices are not limited to books, either; you can use songs, video clips, advertisements, images, and even video games to teach the stances. Your students will quickly understand the concept of resilience if you try to learn one of their video games.

Since the options are so varied, we recommend looking for the following qualities when choosing a text to use in a guided inquiry:

- **Relevant:** The text must be relevant to your students. Use a picture book they adore, a song they can't stop singing, or a video clip from the most recent blockbuster. Find something that fits with their lives.

- **Accessible:** The text must be something that all of your students can access. Don't choose overly complex texts or challenging, new materials. Go for a text that your students will be able to understand through both words and visuals.
- **Clear:** Make sure you are clear about what part of the text, specifically, is showing the stance you are introducing. It may be just a few pages or images, but you should have the exact components in mind ahead of time.

Malini's choice of *Leonardo the Terrible Monster* met all three of these guidelines. The book was well loved and had already been read and reread in the class; her kindergartners could make meaning from the images alone and support that meaning with the words; and the stance that Malini was introducing clearly matched that precise moment in the text.

Discover the Concept

Just as Malini did, as you lead your students through a guided inquiry, you will want to have them discover the concept on their own. You could explicitly tell students, "Today we're going to study empathy," but research has shown that students have a better understanding of a concept (and of a word that will be very new to most) when they discover it first for themselves.

Of course, you'll want to guide your students to the concept and not simply hope that they will discover empathy or persistence entirely on their own. Malini asked her students, "Why would Leonardo stop wanting to be a monster?!" and then went back to the specific page in question, saying, "I want to go back here. I want to look closely, because this is where he changed." By focusing students' attention on the stance in action, Malini guided them to discover the concept.

Older students—and for that matter, younger students—may have words that match the concept and, by all means, encourage your students to share them. After studying a clip of persistence, you might hear, "It's perseverance!" or "He's never giving up!" These words or ideas are only adding to the collective, social construction of the concept.

Name the Concept

Once your students have discovered and discussed the stance you are introducing, it's time to name it explicitly. John Hattie and Gregory Yates, in *Visible Learning*, write that teachers must balance inquiry with direct instruction: "If you are trying to learn a skill, you need social models coupled with descriptive language to enable you to understand and memorize what you observe" (2013, 78). In this case, by introducing one, specific term and definition to represent the concept, you'll give your class a common understanding from which you can build.

Isabel Beck (2013) has stressed the importance of "student-friendly explanations" of new words. These explanations use only known language and indicate how the word is used. We offered suggestions for definitions to use with students in the previous chapter, but you should think carefully about your class and your students when you're creating your definitions—the known words of a kindergartner might be very different from those of a fifth grader. Before you give your own definition, you should also listen closely as students discuss the stance you are discovering. You can mine their conversations for phrases or words that would make the stance more easily understood and authentic to your class.

Here are some tips for naming the concept:

- Say the word and definition on their own and then again in the context in which they were discovered. "Persistence means you try, try again. Max was persistent when he . . ."
- Have students repeat the word and try it out on their own.
- Draw a quick sketch with a memorable symbol to provide a visual association.

Reflect on and Generalize the Concept

Beck's (2013) research into word acquisition and vocabulary reminds us that very few children will leave your guided inquiry understanding or remembering a new term if they are exposed to it only once or twice, no matter how clear your definition may be. To develop a deep understanding of a word and its associated meaning, students need to think and talk about the word in different contexts. The text you studied as a class provided one context, an introduction, but our goal is for students to use these stances across their days and across their lives. We want them to be able to generalize them into everything that they do.

Over the coming year you'll work to reinforce your students' understanding of each stance (see the section "Reflecting on and Maintaining Growth" later in this chapter for more tips on this), but that work will begin even before you send your children away from the rug. Malini had students turn and talk about a time when they might have "felt someone else's feelings in their hearts." By sharing these experiences, children were shifting from the static nature of a stance in a text to the more dynamic nature of the stance in life. Yes, Leonardo was empathetic to Sam, but *we* can also be empathetic. The benefit of making this shift from the text to real life is twofold: it offers another chance to understand this new term and it gives children the opportunity to see their world through that new, powerful lens.

In the following example, fourth graders discover the stance of resiliency. Without question, they each have had moments in their lives when they have been resilient (standing back up as toddlers, moving to a new school, or even correcting a misspelled word), but when Ms. Allen introduces this new lens, they suddenly have a word to match this stance and the agency to recognize their own resiliency and to use it to their advantage.

Olympians Get Back Up: Window into Fourth Grade

It's late September and Ms. Allen calls the class over to the rug.

"All right, fourth graders," Ms. Allen begins as the class settles in to the meeting area. "We've been spending the last few weeks exploring what it means to be optimistic and what it means to be flexible. We've seen just how quickly taking on these two tools can really change our learning. The energy in this classroom for learning is incredible! And it's not even October yet!"

Ms. Allen gestures up to the two charts on the whiteboard. The charts are labeled "Optimism" and "Flexibility" and are covered with sticky notes detailing times that students have tried or witnessed other students using these stances (see Figure 4.1). A third chart hangs next to them, entirely blank.

- Providing opportunities (like charts with sticky notes) for children to record and celebrate times they have used a stance will integrate them into the classroom culture.
- Be sure to link each new stance with the ones that have already been introduced. That way, students will see how the stances weave and work together.

"This time of year, I start to gear up for winter and get excited to start skiing. I was thinking back to last winter and remembering how great it was to watch the Olympics. Did you guys watch, too?"

Ms. Allen looks around the circle and the students nod.

"Yeah!" Addison calls out. "Some of that skiing was so intense!"

"Well, I started thinking about what it takes to be an Olympian. What does it take to grow to be one of the very top athletes in a sport? I'm sure you have to have optimism—you have to think, 'I can try this!' And we know you have to take risks. You probably also have to be flexible. If one type of training or technique doesn't work out for you, you have to try another. But what else? I pulled up this

FIGURE 4.1 Charts on Optimism and Flexibility with Sticky Notes

video—it's an advertisement, really—and I think it will give us a clue about what else Olympians need to have to really be successful."

- Make the resources that you use authentic and accessible to your students. Books—especially picture books—are useful for all ages, but you might want to try using clips, video games, articles, or songs that are especially relevant to your students *and* the stance you are teaching. (For more resources, see Appendix E.)
- When introducing the new inquiry, link the day's work back to the work that has come before it and the ultimate goal: creating energized and engaged learners.

Ms. Allen switches off the lights and pulls up a video clip: an advertisement that played over and over again the previous year.

"Pull out your inquiry notebooks and open to a blank page. Let's watch it with this question in mind: 'What does it take to be an Olympian?' We'll watch the whole thing through twice and then talk about what we've discovered."

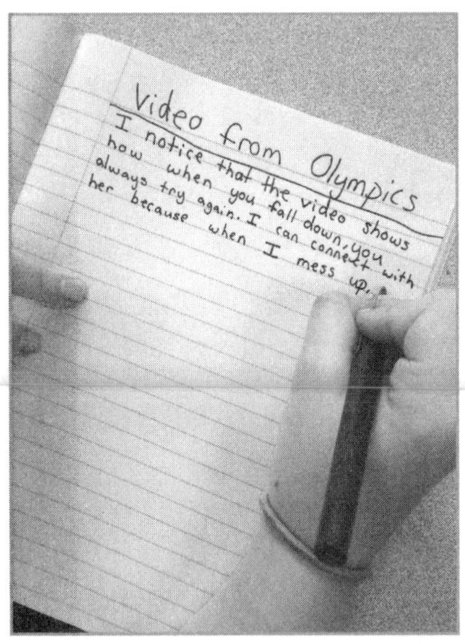

FIGURE 4.2 Inquiry Notebooks: Discovering Resilience

Ms. Allen starts the video. The clip depicts babies, then toddlers, then school-age children, and then young adults falling repeatedly while learning to walk, while just starting their sports, and as professional athletes. The clip concludes with several of the athletes winning races and thanking their moms for "teaching [them] that falling only makes [them] stronger."

Ms. Allen shows the video twice, pausing in between each viewing to restate the inquiry question. The students jot down sketches and notes in their inquiry notebooks (see Figure 4.2).

After the second viewing, Ms. Allen switches the lights back on.

"So," she asks, "what does it take to be an Olympian? Turn and talk to your inquiry partner. What did you notice?"

The children turn to their partners and an energized buzz fills the room. Ms. Allen circulates among the children, listening in and jotting notes.

- Your goal as you circulate is not to hear the word for the concept you are exploring (in this case, *resilience*), but rather to hear students talking about the concept. In this case, you'd want to hear: Olympians get back up and try again.
- Inquiry partners (or small groups) and notebooks are structures that are easily put in place that can help foster deep thinking and reflection.

"All right, fourth graders, let's come back together. Let's get into our circle and start a conversation: What does it take to be an Olympian?"

Ms. Allen uncaps a marker and sits next to the blank piece of chart paper. She looks around the classroom.

"You have to fall and get back up. A lot," Nathaniel begins. "Falling down makes you stronger and you learn from your mistakes."

Ms. Allen takes notes on the chart paper as the children continue the discussion.

"I agree," Amanda says. "No matter how many times you fall, no matter how many times you get hurt, you just keep trying."

"You have to get back up if you want to get better at something. You can't just lie there," Addison said.

Ms. Allen draws a line under the notes on the chart paper. "Let's pause for a second here," she says. "There's a name for this concept that you've discovered. It's called resilience. Thumbs up if you've heard that word before."

A few thumbs go up, but not many.

"Resilience means bouncing back when something goes wrong and trying to learn from your mistakes. We saw those Olympians do it again and again. They fell down, they got back up, and they learned from their mistakes. Let's think about our own learning and growth. What can we learn from Olympians? When have we been resilient? When can we bounce back and learn from our mistakes? Take a moment to turn and talk with your partner about a few times that you've been resilient—in sports, at school, or maybe when learning something new. Go ahead."

- Be sure to give a clear, developmentally appropriate definition for the stance you are introducing. The same definition might not necessarily be the best for kindergartners and middle schoolers, but the concept will be.
- By giving children an opportunity to talk about the concept right away with a partner, you are helping them reinforce both the new idea and the vocabulary word that you will be using all year.

"So what do you think?" Ms. Allen asks, pulling the class back together. "When could we be resilient?"

"I was resilient the first time I tried to do tricks on skis," Cody says.

"When I was five, and I was learning to ride a two-wheeler, I crashed all of the time. But I kept getting back on my bike," Amanda shares.

Ms. Allen jots the two examples on sticky notes and sets them aside.

"Do you think being resilient could help us in school? How so?" Ms. Allen asks.

"Maybe," James suggests, "if you're trying to solve a super hard math problem, you keep trying even if you get it wrong. You could try a different strategy. Then you would be resilient."

"Or," Addison adds, "if you're reading and you keep messing up on a word, you don't just skip it, you figure it out."

"That's resilience?" Ms. Allen asks.

"Yep. That's resilience."

- When you're collecting examples of the new stance, accept both those from school and those from life outside of school. All will be helpful as children make sense of the concept.
- The more students can use the word (hear it, read it, use it themselves), the faster it will become a part of their working vocabulary.

"This video showed moms helping their children up over and over again. And it's true that sometimes it's helpful to have someone help you bounce back. Do you think it has to be your mom?"

"No," Nathaniel says, "it could be a dad, or a friend, or a teacher, or *you*!"

"Yeah," Amanda adds. "It can't always be someone else. It has to be you, too, because you decide if you want to do it again. You have to decide if you want to solve your problems or to keep trying, trying and not give up. It has to be you."

- Take every opportunity you can to have students see themselves as agents of their own learning. (See more about this in Chapter 1.)
- If, during this guided inquiry, the conversation veers off course or students are misunderstanding the concept or the word, quickly steer it back on course. You could say, "That's an interesting idea, but remember that resilience is all about making mistakes, bouncing back, and learning from your mistakes." You may choose to reframe the student's idea with this lens if you can do so quickly and in the moment.

"Fourth graders," Ms. Allen says, "it's time for us to officially add a third tool to our tool kits: resilience." She writes the word and draws the key symbol on the blank chart paper that hangs next to the charts for optimism and flexibility.

"Every time you find yourself or you notice someone else being resilient—bouncing back from a mistake and learning from it—let's add it to our chart. I'll start by adding the examples we came up with today. Make sure to be on the look-out for more!"

Reflecting on and Maintaining Growth

For us, as teachers, the summer months are filled with possibility. We keep notes in journals, bookmark blog posts that inspire us, and envision the classrooms we will inhabit in the upcoming school year. These daydreams are great and powerful; research even tells us that daydreams are healthy and helpful in that they happen when we are in our best creative problem-solving mode (Fries 2010). Yet as every September fades into October, at least one of these aspirations has faded away. So how do we build a successful habit? According to Scott H. Young, author of the essay "Reprogramming Your Daily Habits" (2013), the answer lies in understanding the limits of willpower.

Young refers to research conducted by Roy Baumeister that demonstrates that every person has a finite amount of willpower. When you use it up, it is as though you have drained your gas tank, and it can replenish only over time. Ever have an exhausting day at work? This phenomenon explains why it was then probably harder to complete a normal workout, for example, on that day. You, as the colloquialism goes, ran out of steam. Young goes on to say that you should not combine new complex things at once if you really want to stick to your new habits. If you want to build a new hard habit, take on one at a time. So what does this mean in the classroom?

To help children build these stances, you may first want to ask them to apply them in areas of the day that are somewhat familiar to and "easy" for children in order to avoid draining their "willpower tank" too quickly. In the primary grades, this means play. It will be easier to build a habit of optimism in the art center, which will then transfer to work in reading, writing, and math, than vice versa (see Figure 4.3). In upper-elementary grades, you can choose one core academic area (writing, math, or reading) and then have your students discover how each stance fits in with that specific part of the day. Many will have aha moments or will begin to change their engagement in that academic area. Once you have introduced the stances in writing, for example, you can introduce them in math and reading. Don't shy away from pulling in examples from older students' lives outside of school—their sports, games, music, and weekend adventures are perfect fodder for deepening their understanding of the stances. Just remember: it can be a bit like trying to juggle and ride a bike at the same time when you attempt to launch everything at once. Be patient, keep in tune with your class, and incorporate one thing at a time.

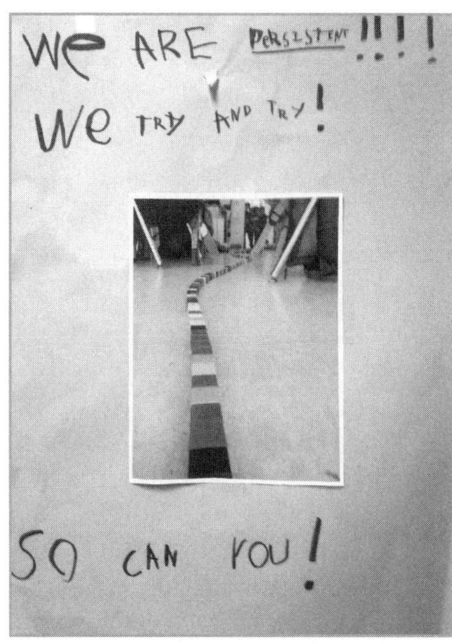

FIGURE 4.3 A Cube Structure in a Classroom Chart Inspires Us to Be Persistent in More Ways

Additionally, we need to commit to and be consistent with our new habit, Young states. Following you will find some simple ways to integrate awareness and reflection on these new stances to promote a high level of consistency.

Check in Regularly with Each Stance

- **Chart:** Make a chart for each stance with a symbol, a visual, and a definition. Leave space at the bottom to add stickies with descriptions, sketches, or photographs of children "living" the stance. (See Figure 4.4.)

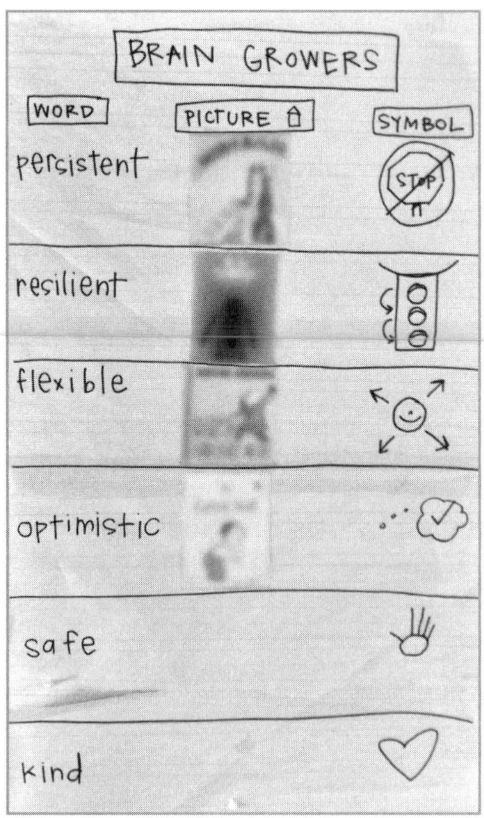

FIGURE 4.4 A Classroom Chart Shows the Variety of Stances

- **Use props or icons:** Visuals will help the class reflect on and remember a stance and what it means to use it. In some primary grades, teachers gave a crown with a visual of the symbol to a child who had demonstrated a stance (see Figure 4.5), and in many grades, children coded work with the symbols of the stances when they used them successfully (see Figure 4.6).

Check in Regularly with the Ecosystem of the Classroom

At the heart of this work is not just individual growth but a community of growth and kindness. We are not advocating "rat race junior," where children persist to outperform peers; rather, we are looking to build a community of common language and living so that we, and the people in our community, can grow and thrive. To that end, it is worth revisiting and reflecting on the community and how we can use these stances to support others.

- **Role-Play:** Use the different stances in role-playing so children can experience what each means. You might role-play different stance approaches to the same problem to see which is most effective or to illustrate differences. For example, if the block tower fell down, what would it mean to be persistent (rebuild it the same way), flexible (build something different), or empathetic (help the person whose blocks fell down because you know how it feels)?
- **Share:** At the end of work time, children can tell about how others used specific stances to help themselves be the best version of themselves.
- **Coach:** Give opportunities for partners to help each other use the stances. You can whisper to a partner that he can help his friend by reminding him to "be flexible" or "be optimistic."

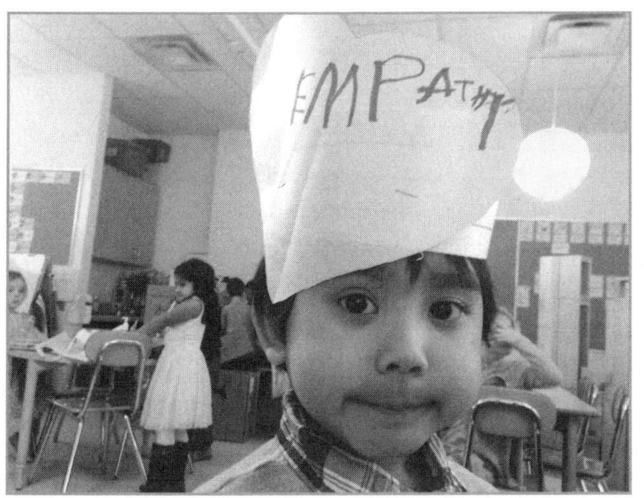

FIGURE 4.5 A Child with an Empathy Crown

FIGURE 4.6 A Piece of Writing Marked with a Symbol for Flexibility

The commitment of a small amount of time each day brings the consistency needed to move an awareness of the stances to a habit of the mind. The following chapters will help you build, refine, and expand the ways you and your students use these stances and understand what it means to be an energized and engaged learner.

SUGGESTIONS FOR ENGAGING FAMILIES

- Invite parents to read the research! Many parents have told us the books we suggested (see Appendix A) have helped them in their own lives, as well as in their parenting.
- Ask parents to talk through times they have (or have not) used these stances in everyday occurrences. Talking through their own adult processes can provide a model for children to follow when they face their own small challenges.
- Invite parents to use these thinking tools (and the language) to celebrate when their children have overcome challenges! Zipping a coat, tying a shoe, and sticking with a hard piano piece are all worthy of remembrance.

Self-Talk: Creating Habits of Resilience by Teaching Productive Inner Dialogue

Like it or not, we each have a voice inside of our head. This voice is a combination of all the voices we have heard through the years, the good ones and the bad. It can be instructive, as when remembering the directions to get to a new location; it can be destructive, like the berating you give yourself when you forget your keys for the hundredth time; it can be your best friend, and it can be your worst enemy. We often tune out our self-talk to a steady hum in the background until moments of stress, when we turn it up. Think of a time recently when you were under stress, not necessarily bad stress, just a time when you were working harder than usual. What was your inner dialogue? Did you give useful tips and encouraging advice? Were your actions accompanied by nagging doubt and fear? Sometimes the only thing that stops us is us—that little voice in our mind that says: *You can't*. The shocking thing is that we are in charge of that little voice, and when we discover we have the power to change our self-talk, we can change our life. We can also help our students develop internal voices that help them instead of holding them back.

One fall Christine was in the middle of a rock-climbing route when she found herself engaging in a downward spiral of negative self-talk. Halfway up the rock face and gazing up at the next move, she said to herself, "This move looks really hard," and then, "I'm not going to make it." And then she thought, "I don't have the upper-body strength, so if I try it, I'll fall." She began to envision her hand grasping at a hold and then slipping. Like a self-fulfilling prophecy, this negative self-talk was affecting every aspect of the challenge at hand: Christine's motivation (Why are you doing this, anyway? Why not head home and eat dinner?), her confidence (You're not this good, are you?), and the act of climbing itself (Feel your arms shaking? Isn't your foot slipping?). In the middle of this spiral, she realized its danger. Taking a breath and closing her eyes, Christine decided to shift to positive self-talk, just to see what would happen. Her self-talk started off generally: "You can do this" and "You've done hard moves like this before." But as she continued, the self-talk became more specific to the climb: "Right hand up to that ledge; trust your feet" and "Breathe, balance, left foot and left hand up. Go for it." Christine found that the more she engaged in instructive, positive self-talk, the more strategic and successful her climbing became.

The power of self-talk—both negative and positive—is evident in our lives every day. It is clear that one of these voices is going to be a better ally to children as they develop and learn. So how do we develop the positive self-talk that enables children to leverage the constellation of stances and to overcome difficulty?

Laying the Neural Roadways That Lead to Productive Self-Talk

Critical to our understanding of self-talk is the understanding that we build neural pathways that promote the self-talk we use the most. Much like highways are built on ancient paths that have been used for hundreds of years, our brains create high-speed connections around our most common types of thinking. In her book *How to Stay Sane*, Philippa Perry references self-observation as a way to change patterns of thought, stating, "the neural pathways that promote toxicity will be used less and will gradually shrink, while those that promote empathy and awareness will grow" (2009, 36). Luckily for us as teachers, the children we teach are in the process of constructing these neural pathways, and it is much less about unlearning and shrinking and much more about helping children lay down the highways in the most productive and positive places.

Talking Is Thinking

Vygotsky believed that children become capable of thinking *as* they talk, meaning thinking and talking are the same for the very young, and speech becomes a tool with which to better understand and clarify what is going on in their minds. Once children reach this point, Vygotsky referred to this as "private speech" (Bodrova and Leong 2007, 68). We should listen closely to what children *say* because it is a powerful indicator of what they will later *think*. A teacher who promotes a certain kind of talk is simultaneously promoting a certain kind of thinking.

> Alexander Luria, a colleague of Vygotsky, argues that private speech actually helps children make their behavior more deliberate (Luria, 1969). In a series of experiments Luria found that general directions, such as "Squeeze two times," did not have an effect on the behavior of young children. Children would squeeze any number of times. However, when children were taught to say "Squeeze, squeeze" and this private speech was directly paired with action, the private speech helped children to control their behavior. (Bodrova and Leong 2007, 69)

Let's try this. If we want to make ourselves squeeze a ball two times, most of us will still need to activate a brief moment of self-talk, stating, "Squeeze, squeeze," or "One, two," to actually complete the direction. Luria's research demonstrates that there is a difference in a child's action when you say something *to* a child and say something in a way that mimics a child's private speech (Bodrova and Leong 2007, 69). It is the difference between saying to a child, "Sound out the word," and saying, "Say the word out loud, listen, and feel the sound. What letter makes that? OK, write that down. Now say the word again . . ." It is not always enough to give a direction; often we need to mimic the self-talk that a young child needs to complete the direction in order to influence behavior. This is true of sounding out words, squeezing balls, and talking oneself through a failure.

As children age, this audible self-talk becomes internalized. Vygotsky described the process as twofold: first children develop inner speech, which then leads to verbal thinking. In Vygotsky's definition, inner speech is what children would previously say out loud to themselves, but they just no longer need to verbalize it to hear it (Bodrova and Leong 2007, 70). Verbal thinking is when the pathway laid down by private speech and inner speech becomes a superhighway. At this point, the thinking becomes so fast and has so many shortcuts (e.g., cutting the pronouns and leaving out whole phrases) that children (and adults) are not even aware of how they got to the thought they have at any given moment. For example, a young child will verbalize the steps to tying a shoe, but adults do it seemingly without conscious thought. However, an adult's mind is still thinking about tying a shoe. The mind is quickly cueing the body through the steps, so quickly it's often not recognized that this is the same thinking process the child is going through but shortened and streamlined after repeated use.

This thinking, because it originated as private speech, can be teased back out into language and studied and manipulated; hence the name *verbal* thinking. When they need to, most adults can slow down their shoe tying and explain it to a child, and adults can learn to tie their shoes differently by substituting one step for another. Shoe tying is not like breathing; it is something we learned, and therefore we can explain it to others and change it if we need to. These are the thoughts we can describe and give words to because they began as things we said aloud to ourselves or things that were said to us.

Deconstructing Superhighways of Doom

Both Vygotsky and Philippa Perry draw the same conclusion: once the superhighway has been laid down, writing and reflecting on the route of any thought is the only way to understand how you got it. When a child has developed negative internal chatter, and that internal chatter has become a fast-moving highway, the teacher and the child have to first deconstruct the negative neural pathway and reroute a more positive pathway through spoken self-talk, then private speech. Only once the new positive pathway has been intentionally set, and the person repeatedly guides him- or herself down it multiple times, can it become a new, better superhighway.

Consider unlearning a bad habit and relearning a new one. For Kristi, it was her sidearm throw in baseball. Correcting her form took a constant vigilance as she reset her body and her mind to the new position, as opposed to the ease of her old stance. Only after weeks and weeks of intentional and thoughtful correction did Kristi realize that her form had altered and her accuracy and speed had improved along with it.

The same principles apply to the voice in your head. It is never too late to make it your greatest ally and the source of the productivity and happiness in your life. For adults and children alike, it is never too early and never too late to lay or relay these neural highways.

THE POWER OF THE PRONOUN

Eric Kross of the University of Michigan studied the pronouns people use when engaging in self-talk. He found that when they used the pronoun *I* it often added additional stress, but that "a subtle linguistic shift—shifting from 'I' to your own name—can have really powerful self-regulatory effects" (Starecheski 2014). Kross conducted a study where he gave people only five minutes to prepare for a speech. He asked some people to address themselves as *I* and some to address themselves in the third person. He found that people who addressed themselves by their names were more likely to engage in positive, supportive inner dialogue. By using the third person, participants were more likely to talk to themselves as a rational, caring friend, and that small distance left no voice for an emotional spiral of negativity.

Using Conferences and Small-Group Work to Support Positive Self-Talk

Chapter 1 outlines, roughly, how the brain works (see page 9); you can use this explanation to help children understand how their brains work. This understanding of neurons and neural pathways can come in handy when we talk about self-talk. Children understand things that are concrete, and, much like children can imagine building a block structure in lots of different ways, we can help them imagine building their own brains in the most productive ways possible. When we teach children to think about their thinking, we give them the keys to a lifetime of self-reflection and growth. The work of developing positive and productive self-talk is best done in small groups or one-on-one.

Many teachers feel comfortable with pulling small groups of children together based on academic needs, but it may feel odd to think about pulling a small group of children together to work on their optimism and their self-talk. However, there is a very real group of children in your classroom who need exactly that! You may see them as the nonstarters in math, the doodlers in writing, the stare-out-the-window readers.

Leaning on the research of Vygotsky, Luria, and Perry, we suggest a spiraling sequence of instruction when building and rebuilding constructive self-talk. We call this a spiraling structure because until this thinking becomes second nature, you may find that you need to revisit certain steps in the process again and again. One thing to keep in mind throughout this process is that it is not this *or* academic support. A better understanding of content and more streamlined thinking will be happy by-products of increased productive self-talk. Before we lay out the steps that lead to these positive and productive self-talk superhighways, we will look in on a classroom in the midst of developing these very skills.

Fostering Flexibility with Positive Self-Talk: Window into Third Grade

Ms. Troncoso scans the classroom as pencils fly across index cards. The children are solving the math equation 6 × 5 by drawing sketches, writing explanations, and crossing out mistakes. It is the first week of multiplication instruction and the excitement in the classroom is palpable.

Ms. Troncoso walks quietly around the room and looks at the children carefully, asking herself, "Who is stuck and stalled? Who is stuck and still working?"

Ms. Troncoso pauses to watch Kate, who is bent over her work. Kate quickly erases one array model drawing and starts another.

From across the room, Ms. Troncoso can see that Matt has written and crossed out several numbers and is now fiddling with a piece of paper and staring out the window at the falling snow. Ms. Troncoso jots Matt's name down on a sticky note.

She circles over to Elise and Laura and sees that they each have a first attempt at solving the equation on their cards. Elise is biting her lip, glancing around the classroom furtively, and Laura is skip-counting on her fingers, staring across the room with narrowed eyes. Ms. Troncoso adds Elise's name to her sticky note.

- The power of teacher observation cannot be overstated. The teacher is gaining important information by watching the class with specific questions in mind (e.g., Who is stuck and stalled?).
- By gathering this information at the end of a lesson, Ms. Troncoso is getting ready to plan for an explicit small group that she will pull together the following day.

When the children complete the exit task, which assesses the day's learning, Ms. Troncoso says, "Mathematicians, remember, this is new and we're all growing at this and learning, every day. The important thing is you worked as hard as you possibly could."

Ms. Troncoso gathers the exit tasks as her students scurry out the door for recess. She glances through them quickly and notes who had strategies to solve the problem, who tried repeatedly and failed, and who tried once and abandoned the problem.

On John's exit task she notices that he tried to find the answer with repeated addition but crossed out his work completely. She pulls out her sticky note and adds John's name to her list.

- Using multiple sources of data is both more reliable and more practical. In busy classrooms it's helpful to have many ways to see what your students know to determine how to pull your groups together.
- The teacher will use these exit tasks to form several small groups, some on content and strategies and others on habits of learning.

That afternoon Ms. Troncoso thinks carefully about what, exactly, would help her students' progress the most. She thinks about these students as mathematicians (John, Elise, and Matt have strong number sense and a good mathematical footing) and, more generally, as learners with habits (each of these students seems to give up if the first strategy doesn't work). Ms. Troncoso plans a small group on self-talk to promote flexibility. She jots down notes and sketches a plan for a chart she will have the students collectively create.

The next day, while the rest of the class is engaged in building area models of multiplication equations with their math partners, Ms. Troncoso pulls the group together at her meeting table. "You have been doing such hard work this week with starting multiplication! It may feel scary when you try something for the first time. Sometimes our brains get uneasy, and if we try something one way and it doesn't work, we just want to stop and give up. Have you noticed that?"

- Acknowledging the challenging nature of the work students are engaged in helps them see that their struggling is important, that it can be productive, and that it can lead to new learning.

Matthew nods his head. John shrugs his shoulders. Elise says, "Yeah. Sometimes I just get so tired I want to just give up."

Ms. Troncoso nods her head. "I feel the same way sometimes," she says. "Today I pulled you together because I want to teach you that, sometimes, if we have tried one way of solving a problem and it doesn't work, our brain gets recharged by trying a completely different way of doing something. All we need to do is to give ourselves a reminder and say, 'This way isn't working. How can I switch it up?' Watch me give it a try."

- Giving students a specific phrase, such as "switch it up," makes this learning easier to replicate.

Ms. Troncoso pulls out a whiteboard, a marker, and an eraser.

"Let's pretend that I'm trying to solve three times twelve. I've tried skip-counting by threes, but I'm getting all muddled up. But am I going to give up?" Ms. Troncoso raises her eyebrows and glances over at the students.

"Nope," they chorus.

▸ The more you work with your students on persistence, the more quickly they will adopt the mindset that you simply don't give up after trying something once. The challenge becomes giving them the tools and strategies to help them persist.

"Nope," Ms. Troncoso echoes. "I'm going to say, 'Switch it up! What could I do differently?' Hmmm. Let me see. Skip-counting didn't work. What if I tried drawing an array model?"

Ms. Troncoso quickly sketches a model and solves the problem.

"Hey!" she says. "Look at that! I told myself, 'Switch it up! What could I do differently?' and it worked! I figured it out."

She hands out whiteboards to each of the students. "Now it's your turn. Try out this self-talk with eight times eight. Remember, when you feel stuck, say out loud, 'Switch it up!' and then try another way of solving the problem."

John quickly starts sketching out an array. He points to each of the columns and starts skip-counting, "Eight, sixteen, twenty-four, thirty-two, . . . ," he pauses. "Thirty-, thirty- . . . where was I?"

John looks up at Ms. Troncoso. "What can you do?" she asks.

▸ Students will need different levels of scaffolding while practicing this new self-talk. Some will practice it without reminders, others will need to be prompted, and others still will need to have the phrases repeated again.

"Switch it up!" John says. He erases his work and starts writing multiples of eight on his board.

Ms. Troncoso turns to Matt. "OK," he says, erasing his work. "I guess it's time to try another way! I'll switch it up!"

Ms. Troncoso smiles. "Keep at it!"

Elise caps her marker and looks over her work. "Got it!" she says, pleased.

"You sure did, Elise. You didn't come to any trickiness when you were solving that problem. But since today we're practicing what to do when we *do* run into something challenging, do you think you could pretend? Just for practice?"

▸ It is not a given, in the small-group context, that students will run into the tricky situation needed to practice the self-talk strategy. In these cases, have students "play" stuck. Most will happily take on the role, and the experience from the rehearsal will serve them well when they are on their own.

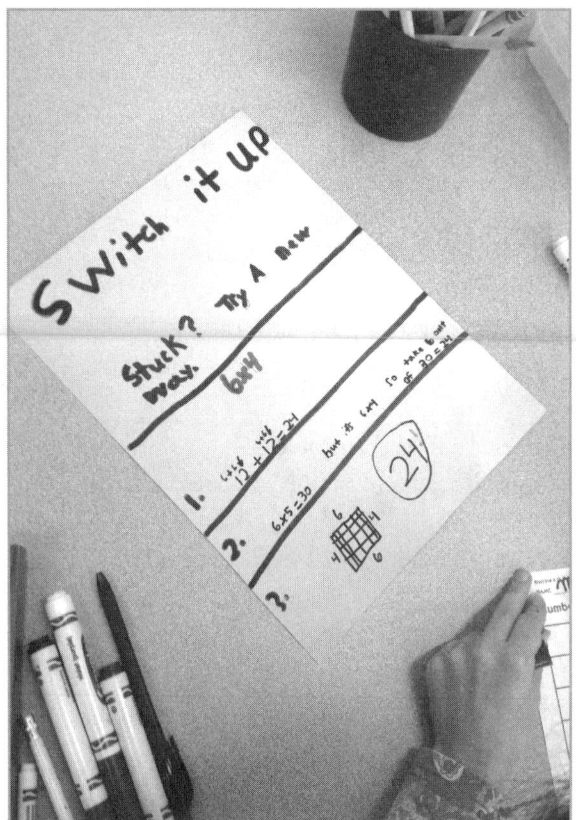

FIGURE 5.1 Switch It Up: Students Created a Chart to Support a Self-Talk Strategy That Promotes Flexibility

Elise nods. She looks down at her work again. "Oh no!" she says, dramatically. "It's all wrong!" She pretends to erase it as she says, "I won't give up. I'll switch it up and try another strategy. I can do this."

Ms. Troncoso pulls the group back together.

"Today," she tells the students, "you practiced something very important to your learning. You practiced reminding yourself to be flexible when your brain is challenged. Can I put the three of you in charge of creating a chart that's called 'Switch It Up'? Maybe you could have different multiplication strategies on it and we could hang it in our math center as a reminder." (See Figure 5.1.)

After math that morning, Ms. Troncoso asks the three group members to show her, on their hands, how many times they told themselves to "switch it up" or to "try another way."

"Wow!" she says. "I wonder, could you be on the lookout for the rest of the day of other times where you could say that to yourself? Let's check in before you take off this afternoon."

- This teacher has created three means for reinforcing the work the children did in their small group: a tool, a quick reflection, and an opportunity for students to reflect on the transference of this strategy.
- These students are taking on the role of "switch it up" experts and can use their expertise to guide their own learning and that of their peers.

Moving from Idea to Action

The impact of self-talk, positive or negative, is revealed in our words and in our deeds. What we do or don't do in any given situation has much to do with what our inner voice says to us. When we harness the power of that voice, our life becomes more intentional and more under our own control. Ms. Troncoso gave this knowledge, and its power, to her students. The next chapter will help you do the same.

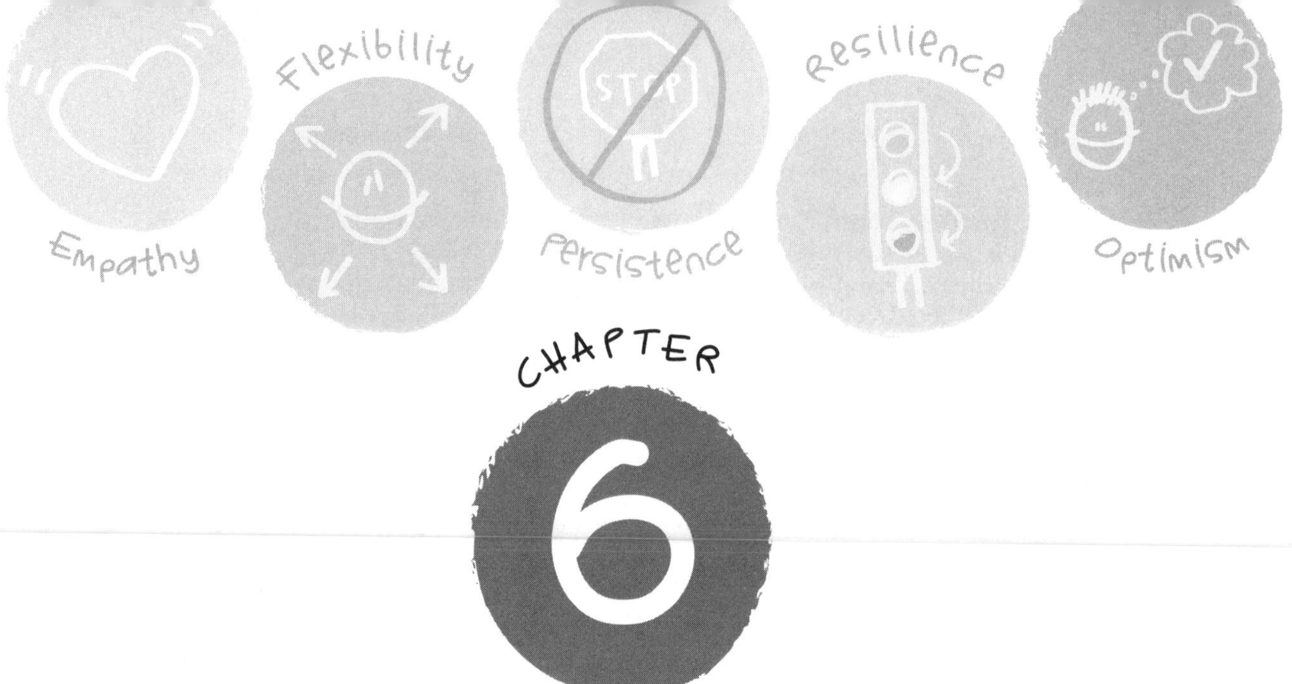

Using Small Groups to Teach Productive Self-Talk

Runners have known the power of self-talk for years. Often runners adopt a mantra to repeat as they run, especially when the running gets tough. In fact, Kristi's is "If I can walk, I can run." In the *Runner's World* article "The Magic of Mantras," by Christie Aschwanden, sports psychologist Stephen Walker explains that he teaches mantras to help athletes "direct [their] mind away from negative thoughts and toward a positive experience" (2011). The article goes on to quote David K. Ambuel, a philosophy professor: "Indeed, the Sanskrit word 'mantra' literally means 'instrument for thinking.' As such, these short words or phrases have long been used to focus the mind in meditation." If runners are being taught mantras to overcome mental challenges on the course, can we not do the same in our classrooms? As with running, sometimes the biggest obstacle to learning is our own mind.

In Your Own Classroom

It can feel surprising when you realize that some children do not need more content, but rather more experience with how learning feels and how to work through mistakes and challenges in productive ways. You may now be rethinking some of the behaviors that you've seen from students, as Ms. Troncoso did in the previous chapter, and wondering, "What were those children thinking, and how could I help such children best?"

In the third-grade example in Chapter 5, and in the kindergarten example later in this chapter, the teachers follow a four-step process. This process, as seen in the example in Chapter 5, may be split up across the day but ultimately will not take more than ten minutes of time.

1. Observe.
2. Gather your group.
3. Teach—model, let children practice, and create a tool.
4. Reflect and share.

Start with Observation

To begin, observe your class with these questions in mind (for more on observation, see Chapter 2):

- Who gets started right away? Who doesn't? (optimism for the task)
- Who gets stuck and stalled? (flexibility and persistence)
- Who looks to be hiding his or her work? (resilience)

Talk to your students:

- What are you thinking as you try this?
- What could you say to yourself to help yourself out of trouble?
- How do you feel right now?

Study the work:

- Who tried only once?
- Who crossed out or erased his or her work excessively?
- Who spent a lot of time on one small aspect of the task?

Gather Your Group

As you plan your small group or conference, you will want to pick a specific trait and specific phrase of self-talk to model. The table "Self-Talk That Supports Different Traits" will help you narrow down what a child needs and determine what self-talk may best help that child or group. Next, you will need to decide if you would like to ground your group in a specific area—for example, writing, math, blocks, or reading—or if the instruction will remain more general. The benefit of grounding the small group in a specific content area, as Ms. Troncoso chose to do, is that the modeling of the self-talk can be more concrete and may lead to easier application. However, our goal as teachers is for students to be able to transfer these traits and habits to all areas of their lives. To this end, you may want to model, for example, how a specific self-talk phrase can help you be flexible in writing, math, and art, or, as in the example in the previous chapter, have children set a personal goal to continue to use the talk you have taught. (For more on goal setting, see Chapters 9 and 10.)

As the building of this self-talk habit is a spiraling practice, it lends itself well to one-on-one or one-on-two conferring scenarios. Some of your best opportunities for instruction will be in the heat of the moment when students are trying to overcome a challenge in choice time, in their reading, or at snack. Snatch up these moments and think intentionally about what you will teach and how you will teach it. The "Building Blocks of Positive Self-Talk" section later in this chapter can help you envision how this will look similar and different.

Teach the Concept

Begin your teaching by taking an opportunity to remind students of the importance of this "brain work." The more aware they are of their role in their learning, the better they will be able to engage in these habits and, indeed, in their learning. Ms. Troncoso did this with a quick question: "Should I give up?"

Model

Next, model a scenario in which you encounter a challenge, and narrate as you go with positive self-talk. Sometimes your instruction will be the steps of a skill, but within these steps, you will want to embed the phrase or phrases of the trait you are teaching. A simple, catchy phrase like "Switch it up!" will be easy for children to repeat to themselves as they work and is precisely what Luria spoke of when he altered his language from "Squeeze two times" to "Squeeze, squeeze" (Bodrova and Leong 2007, 69).

Let Children Practice

Then you will want children to replicate this positive self-talk. Their self-talk will be most productive if they learn the power inherent in what they say to themselves. One of the most important aspects of these small groups is practicing saying self-talk phrases out loud. Children—even older children—are natural players and will

Self-Talk That Supports Different Traits

Observation	Stance to Target	Example Self-Talk
A child isn't starting the work. A child says he or she is "thinking" for a long period.	***Optimism***	• I have done it before; I can do it again! • I can try; the worst I can do is fail! • I can try; let's see what happens! • I know the steps to start; let me say them again. • I can use tools in the classroom; let me look at them to get started.
A child scribbles over or obliterates his or her work. A child throws out work or continually restarts. A child says the work is "boring."	***Resilience***	• I made a mistake; it happens. I can look it over and see what I can change. • That was disappointing, but let me try again; I might get it next time. • That didn't work at all! I will try something else. • I am going to take some time away and come back to this. • Let me think about the steps again. Which one could I change?
A child tries one way and then is stuck. A child has made only one attempt at a task. A child says, "I'm done," very quickly.	***Flexibility***	• What options do I have? • That way isn't working; what else can I do? • What are all the ways I could solve this? • Let me look at the tools in the classroom to help me think of options.
A child has very little work. A child works a little and then gets stalled.	***Persistence***	• I am getting frustrated, but if I try again maybe I will get it. • I have gotten over tough spots before; I just need to stick with it a little longer. • I know the steps; let me do them one more time more slowly.
A child gets upset when he or she doesn't get his or her way. A child has a hard time collaborating or playing with peers.	***Empathy***	• When this happens to me, I feel . . . I bet he/she feels the same. • I can say or do something kind to show I care. • I will still have a turn even if I don't go first. • I can ask, "What do you need?"

gladly take on the playful role of a student trying to overcome a challenge, as we saw Elise do in the example in Chapter 5. Your scaffolding of their self-talk may need to be explicit; you might say, "Now you practice: say, 'I'll try it again!'" Then it may become less explicit; you might just need to prompt students with a question like "What could you say to yourself right now?" Remember to keep your instruction and their modeling focused on the specific trait and phrases of self-talk you have decided to target. Part of what made Ms. Troncoso's small group so effective is that she did not need to get bogged down in math instruction; she could fully concentrate on helping children be flexible in what they *already* knew.

Create a Tool to Help Children Maintain This Talk

In addition to modeling and practicing, you will want to create a tool with the children in your small group or your conference to help them maintain this self-talk long after your group has finished. These tools can include charts, sticky notes with quick sketches and key phrases, bookmarks, photographs with captions, checklists, and tally cards. Some of these tools might be used by the whole class and others should be personalized for individual learners. (See Figure 6.1.)

Vygotsky calls such a tool a mediator—something that stands as an intermediary between a stimulus (*My first try did not work.*) and an individual response to the stimulus (*Switch it up!*) We create mediators to prompt a specific response (Bodrova and Leong 2007, 51). By sending children off from a small group or conference with a tool, we are helping them to engage and learn independently in situations that previously needed adult guidance.

FIGURE 6.1 Stalled Writing: A Student Who Has a Hard Time Getting Started with Writing Tallies Every Time He Uses a Self-Talk Phrase to Help

Reflect and Share

Reflecting on a newly learned skill is equally as important as practicing the skill. Children who encounter a challenge and then employ self-talk to overcome that challenge will quickly learn the power of their inner voice. Often these moments don't wait for a formal time of reflection, and the children's shouts can be heard echoing across the classroom: "I did it! I tried it again and I got it!" However, by asking children reflective questions such as, "How did you help yourself today?" and "What got you out of this tricky spot?" we are further reinforcing traits like persistence, flexibility, optimism, and resilience.

Reflect

You may choose to have children draw or write about a time over the course of the day that they employed self-talk to overcome something tricky. Some teachers opt to do this at the end of the day or, like in the example in Figure 6.2, at various points throughout the day.

You may also pull the small group back together and have the kids share with each other instances when this self-talk was particularly helpful.

You may want to take this opportunity to elicit from children other areas or scenarios to which this instruction could apply. You might ask, "Where else would it help your brain to say, 'I've done this before; let me try it one more time'?" Just

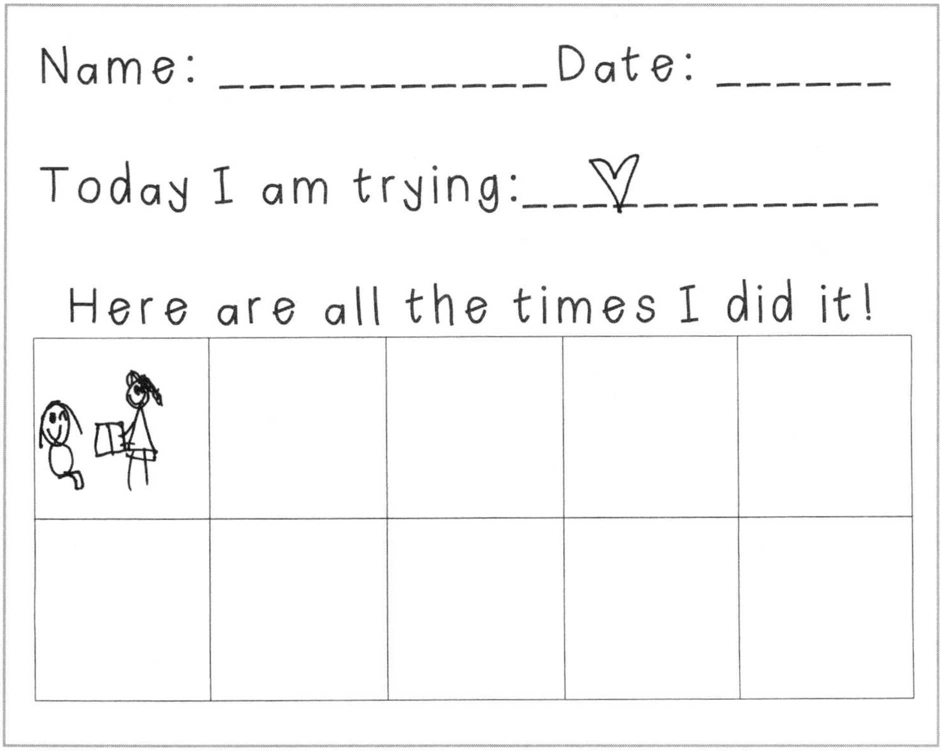

Name: ____________ Date: ______

Today I am trying: __♡________

Here are all the times I did it!

FIGURE 6.2 Kindergarten Reflection: The Child Set a Goal to Be Kind During the Day (Top Line, Represented by a Heart) and Drew a Time When She Was Kind

asking this question elicits reflection and metacognition. You might hear children say, "I could try this when I'm feeling stuck in math, too," or "This is just like when taking a shot in soccer. If I don't get it the first time, I just try it again and again." When we ask children to examine their mental superhighways, we create opportunities for reflection and change.

Share: Teach a Classmate or Group

When students have mastered a specific self-talk strategy, you can provide them with the opportunity to teach a classmate or a small group. You may do this informally, perhaps by asking one student to coach another by sharing her newly created tool and expertise during a tricky moment. Or you may ask students to model their self-talk strategies in a more formal small-group setting, essentially running a replica of the small group they learned in a few days before. By giving students these opportunities, we are providing them with a context to reflect upon and build their own self-talk strategies and those of their peers, and another opportunity to further develop a productive and positive neural pathway. Maria Montessori would argue that it is the ability to teach others that signals true knowing.

Through this reflection and sharing, the whole community is enriched. Children become more sensitive to the self-talk of themselves and others and are able to positively support each other in productive self-talk.

Once you feel comfortable with observing and gathering groups, you may find yourself immersed in teachable moments for productive self-talk. The following story from a kindergarten classroom demonstrates just such an "on the fly" group.

The Building Blocks of Positive Self-Talk: Window into Kindergarten

Things are getting heated between Rosie and Elias.

Their teacher, Meggie, hears the argument rise up above the general hum of this day's choice time workshop and leaves the students she is helping with constructing a cardboard spaceship to investigate. As she weaves around the sand table "bakery" and the blocks "pet shop," she spies a bridge collapse in the city that Elias and Rosie are building.

"I didn't *knock* it down, it *fell* down!" Elias shouts, fists clenched, face red. "I *can't* make it stay up! It keeps *falling*!" With each shouted word, Elias stamps a foot in disbelief and rage.

"Well, let's be persistent then!" Rosie calmly asserts, taking Elias' hand and bringing him back to the bridge. Meggie pauses for a moment, delighted by this turn of events, and is considering whether or not to stop the class to celebrate this moment of growth when she catches the next bit of the encounter.

Elias says, "I was persistent! See?" He puts the block back on top and the bridge falls again. "It just won't work." Rosie takes in this moment and seems perplexed. Persistence, as they understand it, has just failed them.

- Play is a powerful place to have children begin to practice positive self-talk since they are naturally engaged in the challenges play presents.
- This group is gathered in an impromptu, teachable-moment way, unlike pre-planned groups that may also happen throughout the day.

Meggie sweeps in at this moment, as the very defeated Elias and Rosie begin to take the blocks away from the failed bridge to use elsewhere. She grabs them both and starts by validating their feelings.

"Guys, I can see how disappointed you are by the bridge collapse. It feels bad to try something again and again and not have it work." As she talks, the two nod solemnly.

- Though it seems small to us, the bridge collapse is a failure of life's work in a child's mind. When we validate children's feelings, we help them make sense of their own responses.

"Sometimes persistence isn't enough," Meggie goes on. "Sometimes we need to be resilient, which means when something doesn't work we think, 'Hmmm, why?' And then we find the mistake, fix it, and try again!"

- After validating a feeling, you can help a child move past it. We implicitly show our classroom mindset to be "Yes, that was disappointing, but we are not the type of people to be stopped by hard things."
- This is a preview of the self-talk the children will be asked to employ in a moment; repetition is powerful when it comes to building neural pathways.

Meggie sits side by side with Elias and Rosie and ponders the bridge collapse. "Hmm," she wonders aloud, "what happened to make it fall?" She cocks her head to the side thoughtfully, and Elias and Rosie copy her stance, as small children often do. "Can you guys try it one more time, and when it falls, can you watch what happens?"

Elias and Rosie go to put the block on top again and it becomes evident what is happening: the top block is just a little too short to span the distance, so one supporting block is made to lean. When the children release their hands, the support falls, taking down the bridge. As this happens, Meggie says, "Ooooh! What an interesting challenge to sort out! Isn't that interesting? What happened? Let's find it, fix it, and try again."

- Implicitly model that failure is the start of something interesting, not the end.
- Again, repetition is key.
- The teacher is narrating self-talk here.

Rosie and Elias aren't sure, so Meggie prompts them to do it again, saying what they are doing as they do it.

- Repeating the steps of an unsuccessful attempt can sometimes help you find and correct the mistake.
- The teacher is now narrating and asking for replication of her talk.

"I put the block on and then it fell down," Elias states, but Rosie has noticed something. "*Look*!" she yells. When she puts the block on again, she sees that the support tilts.

"What?" Meggie asks.

"It's going sideways and it can't go sideways!" Rosie says, referring to the tilted block.

Meggie says, "Ooh! You found it! At times like this you say: 'Interesting! I can fix that and try again!' Can you try saying that?"

Elias and Rosie repeat after her.

- First the teacher narrated how to approach the challenge; now she is asking the children to repeat after her, much like Luria had the children repeat, "Squeeze, squeeze," to modify their behavior.

Rosie moves the block in slightly, and the bridge stands on its own. Elias high-fives her and they both beam at the bridge. "You did it!" Meggie says. "Can you tell yourself, 'I fixed it!'?" The children repeat it, beaming.

"Whoa," Meggie begins, "I think I can actually see your brains getting bigger! You guys did something *huge* today: you had something hard happen and instead of giving up, you looked closely and found a mistake. Then you were like, 'Interesting! I can fix that and try again!'—and you did!" They nod, and Meggie continues, "Could you guys make a poster about this? Like maybe draw what you did to fix it and give a tip that we find mistakes and fix them?" (See Figure 6.3.)

- The child-constructed chart will serve as a reminder for these students of a way to think about future challenges.
- The chart can also be used to teach others about the way to approach challenges, and it can be used throughout the day to link the concrete experience of play to the work of finding and fixing mistakes in reading, writing, and math.

Reflecting on and Maintaining Growth

Jeremy Dean, psychologist and author of *Making Habits, Breaking Habits* (2013), found that on average it takes sixty-six days to form a habit. However, perhaps more importantly, he found that the difficulty of the habit for an individual predicted how long it would actually take that person to form a habit. Some habits were formed in 50 days, and some took 264 days (7). In short, one small-group lesson will not redefine a child, but a series of small and concerted efforts over time will. For these reasons, some of the most important work comes after the explicit instruction has ceased.

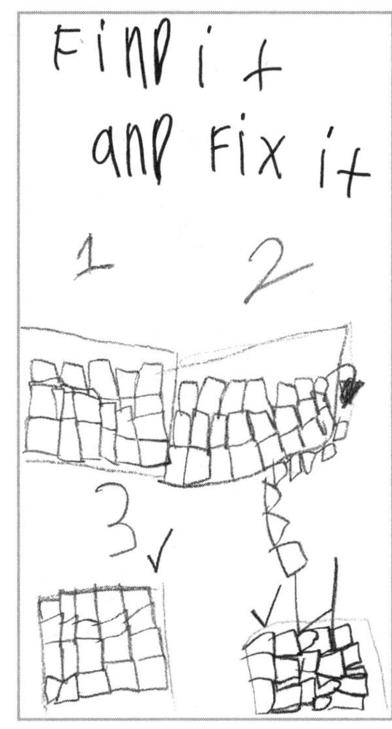

FIGURE 6.3 "Find It and Fix It" Chart

Check in Regularly with Individual Self-Talk

We often keep data on the growth our students show in math, reading, and writing. But what about the growth they show as people? We recommend regular interviews that give you, and your students, feedback on the ways they think about themselves, about challenges, and about their growth.

In the domain of self-talk, we recommend keeping, or have children keep, records of their responses to some of the following questions over time:

- When I (you) get stuck, what do I say to myself?
- What do I (you) do when something feels new or hard?
- What words help me (you) when something is hard? What words hurt me (you)?

When working with young children, you may gather some of this information from observation, since they may not be able to name their own thinking. However, the ways young children talk are the ways they think, so observation will give you an incredibly accurate window into their minds. We often refer back to the notes we take in conversation, saying things like, "You *used* to say you were bored when things were hard, but now I hear you say things like, 'Oh boy! I bet I can do this!'" This small check-in reminds children of the ways they have grown and also gives reinforcement to the growth of the most useful of neural pathways.

With older children, you may carve out time to have them jot down their reflections in a notebook and ask them to notice how they have changed over the course of the school year. You may even offer a chart or a space in your classroom for children to collect and share new self-talk phrases that they create on their own. As children become increasingly metacognitive, you will be amazed at the inventive self-talk they develop. Their quips and slogans (such as "Don't take a brain vacation" and "Grow, brain, grow!") will reflect not only all of the work your students are doing but also the classroom culture they are creating.

Check in Regularly with the Ecosystem of the Classroom

Community meetings, shares throughout the day, and partner times can give you opportunities to maintain and build on the habits in this chapter that you've started laying down.

- **Role-Play:** With partners or larger groups, ask children to role-play a scenario in which someone has a problem. Have the class "be the brain" and say things to help the child through the problem.
- **Share:** Have students tell a partner or the group some ways they talked to themselves to help them out of trouble. Jot down the language so that other children can use it at other times.
- **Coach:** Give opportunities for partners to help each other use positive self-talk. In times when students work with partners, you can listen in to the support partners give each other. You may encourage partners to say not just, "You can do it," but rather "Tell yourself, 'I can do it!'"

These opportunities allow children to practice and perfect the productive self-talk they need to overcome challenges—challenges they will face not only as students but as adults as well.

SUGGESTIONS FOR ENGAGING FAMILIES

The benefit to all of this emphasis on self-talk is that it forces teachers and caregivers to reflect on their own internal dialogue. Often we find that our self-talk is not the most positive and that we, too, have neural pathways we would like to rebuild to lead to more constructive places. The good news is that all of this malleable! The human brain is a remarkable organ, able to adapt, rebuild, and rewire in the most magnificent of ways. To help families support their children's positive inner dialogue, you might invite them to try the following:

- Narrate what they see their child doing with specific directions and the language of the traits. For example:
  - "You are trying the zipper by yourself again! Sometimes it takes more than one try. Grab the handle; now tug; tug again. Don't give up; you are almost there!"
  - "I saw that you tried one strategy to solve that multiplication problem and then tried another when it didn't work for you. That was so flexible of you. Could you try that with this division problem?"
- Narrate their own (positive) thinking when they do something tricky.
- Keep a diary and encourage their child to keep one too! Philippa Perry cites studies that found keeping a diary "positively affect[s] several aspects of the immune system, including T-cell growth and certain antibody responses" (2009, 32). Additionally, keeping a diary helps you discover some of the thinking highways you have built over your lifetime.

Storytelling: Harnessing the Power of Narratives to Shape Identity

Our lives are made up of stories. If we are lucky, we've had people in our lives who have told them to us: the day we were born, the first time we walked or spoke, the moment we started riding our bike on our own. Sometimes the stories we know best are the ones we tell ourselves about our origins, big events in our life, the problem at work yesterday. Stories are the warp and the weft that shape and color our identity.

Kristi had a friend growing up, Anna, whose mom used to often tell Anna how lucky she was to have a sister. Her mom had been an only child and often reflected on the loneliness that had brought her. When Anna and her sister would fight, inevitably her mother would break out a tried-and-true story of playing a board game. By herself. Moving both pieces. It was a rainy summer day, the story went, and her only option in her lonely world was herself. She would pause for a moment, sigh, and stare off into the middle distance. Sometimes she would then add on this line: "That's why I am so much happier being a loner; I am just used to my own company." It was true: when given a chance, Anna's mom preferred her individual pursuits, believing her childhood experiences had programmed her this way.

Her mom's personal narrative of her childhood was unchallenged for decades until several years ago, when Anna's grandmother passed away. There was a dinner. For the first time, Anna met second cousins and cousins that had lived by her mother when she was young and had moved away in their twenties. One cousin in particular told story after story of the hijinks the two of them would get into—the time they thought there was a ghost, the time they almost set fire to the shed, all the sleepovers. As Anna listened and laughed and as her mom chimed in with details, a strange cognitive dissonance settled over her.

"Mom?" Anna asked. "Why do you always say you had no one to play with and no friends when you were young?"

Her mom stopped and a puzzled look crossed her face. "I don't know," she said after a pause. Her bank of childhood stories had no shared space with the stories this cousin told; it was almost as though she had forgotten them until that very moment.

And that is the truly amazing thing about the stories that make us—we are the ones that make them and keep them, even the bad ones. They may not even be true, or they may just be half the story. We have a chance to color every event how we choose.

Turning the Feelings That Break Us into the Stories That Make Us

> *We are what we pretend to be, so we must be careful about what we pretend to be.*
>
> —KURT VONNEGUT, *Mother Night*

Finish this story:

> Once there was a terribly poor princess with not a penny to her name and all alone in the world. She was kind and beautiful, and one day she saw a poor beggar. Though she was poor and hungry, she shared her one scrap of bread with this beggar, who, lo and behold, turned out to be a . . . ?

We are guessing you did not say duck. Probably you said prince, or genie, or some magical creature, which is what we imagined, too. Have you heard this story before? No, of course not. We just made it up. But it certainly *sounds* like a story you have heard before. When you hear stories again and again, like fairy tales, you begin to predict their outcomes using the long-established patterns you have learned. Though this is easy to see with books and movies—how often have we referred to a plot as "so predictable"?—it less easy to see in our own lives.

Imagine you were a child helping two other classmates build a very tall tower of blocks. As you put another high block on, the whole tower fell. As the fruit of your and your classmates' labor lay at your feet, what would you do? What would you think? In part, that answer lies in the stories you have heard (and told) for the whole of your life.

Storytelling and Identity

Societies have creation myths, history books are filled with angled anecdotes, and family histories are often told as series of stories that help us understand our place in the world. We, as people, carry a collection of stories in our minds that help us know who we are and how we act. Phillipa Perry, in her book *How to Stay Sane*, writes:

> Our minds are formed by narratives. . . . Children and their parental figures narrate their experience together and, in doing so, organize their memories and put them in a social context. . . . The co-construction of story has negative and positive outcomes. The downside is that the parental figure can unduly influence the child with his or her own fears, anxieties, prejudices, and restrictive patterns of being; but the upside is that co-forming narratives . . . impart[s] positive values, group culture and individual identity. (2009, 95–96)

The stories we tell and hear, especially those we hear as children, help us to understand who we are in the world. A caregiver or an adult often serves as coauthor and can, unwittingly at times, support or erode a child's self-image based on the details and meaning he helps the child draw from everyday events. It makes sense, if you hear story after story about being a failure, that soon you will tell yourself stories about being a failure. On the flip side, if you hear and tell stories that help you see yourself in positive ways, you will carry those stories with you and begin to tell your own stories of optimism. The events may be the same, but the angle and emotional core of the stories can have different interpretations and different impacts on your self-perception.

It is true that life is filled with ups and downs and it does no one a service to ignore the downs; however, Perry argues, you should try to find the positive spin on the events in your life so that when you confront difficult times in the future, you can face them with hope, not fear. In fact, Perry goes on to write, "if we do not have a mind that is *used* to hearing good news, we do not have the neural pathways to process such news" (2009, 106). Understanding good news has its own neural pathway, like learning to read. People need experience with good news to understand it. When children repeatedly hear stories with resilience, empathy, flexibility, and agency at their core, they grow the neurons that help them find those same stances in novel situations, just as they build the neural pathways of self-talk that we described in Chapters 5 and 6. Children without such experiences do not have the same brain pathways that allow them to know such interpretations exist.

Imagine the next events occurred in the block scenario described earlier: A classmate yelled, "You ruined it!"

A teacher, missing the bulk of the situation, only heard another child saying that you knocked over her blocks. The teacher then pulled you to the side for a time-out, saying, "No knocking over blocks!"

You might at that time begin to tell this story: "We were building blocks and then I ruined it." Now imagine you heard that again and again, and you'll begin to understand why some people believe they ruin everything they touch.

Now imagine a different scenario, one where these same events occurred: A classmate yelled, "You ruined it!"

A teacher, missing the bulk of the situation, only heard another child saying that you knocked over her blocks. This time, instead of passing judgment, the teacher inquired about the sequence of events and helped write a different story. "Trying to build something big and ambitious together and having it fall doesn't mean it is ruined; it just means you have to work together to find a better way. It makes sense to be sad and frustrated that it fell, but after you feel that way for a little while you can try again in a different way, now that you are a little wiser."

You can imagine the ways you might be affected by living through one of these scenarios repeatedly as opposed to the other. The only difference is in the stories that were told about the events that occurred. Teachers can serve as guides, helping children focus their attention on specific details that help lead personal stories toward ones of positivity.

This Is Your Brain on Stories

Adults fill this storytelling and sense-making role all the time for children. When we mirror and retell experiences, we help children make sense of their feelings and their actions. Daniel Siegel and Tina Payne Bryson, in their practical and helpful book *The Whole-Brain Child* (2012), frame this as helping a child integrate her brain, meaning we help all the parts work in coordination. Why does integration matter? According to the authors, when we help all the parts of the brain work together, like left brain and right brain, for example, we strengthen neural connections and allow children to use "their mental resources to full capacity" (9). They go on to say, "An integrated brain results in improved decision making, better control of body and emotions, fuller self-understanding, stronger relationships, and success in school" (10). When we help children build connections between all the parts of their brain, we help them achieve greater success in life.

Storytelling assists in this goal of integration because it brings together the right side of the brain, traditionally seen as the more emotional side, and the left, the more logical side, where language originates. In Siegel and Bryson's words, "To tell a story that makes sense, the left brain must put things in order, using words and logic. The right brain contributes the bodily sensations, raw emotions, and personal memories, so we can see the whole picture and communicate our experience" (2012, 29). Using the logic and language of the left brain gives a name to our feelings and our experience, and that connection is often enough to help a person calm down (29). Think of a time when you had a feeling of dread or anxiety. Its slinky behind-the-scenes impact was your right brain at work. When that happens, we should stop and take the time to put it in words: *I feel like I am dreading something. What could it be? What's coming up? I have had a lot of good things happening; I shouldn't feel dread! Although there was that time when I thought I would get that job and the whole thing came crashing down. . . . I'm probably thinking that this will fall through, too.* It's through this linguistic untangling that we bring worry and emotion into the logical left brain, which allows us to understand and manage our feelings.

Sometimes children construct their own stories based on their egocentric logic, such as "Mommy slammed the door, so she must be mad at me." Helping children put these feelings into words, and helping unkink the logic, is a critical step in helping children overcome fearful or negative associations. Sometimes doors just slam, sometimes mommies are just grumpy, but a child does not always know this, unless you help sort it out. Including the child's input is critical, because you are helping the child make sense of his or her own experience, not telling the child what he or she felt. In Siegel and Bryson's experience (and ours as well), children will want to hear a story again and again, until its power fades.

So why do stories work this magic on us? Daniel Pink, in his book *A Whole New Mind*, states it bluntly: "Stories are easier to remember—because in many ways, stories are *how* we remember" (2005, 101). Since the earliest reaches of time, we have used stories to communicate information to one another. Why this works, Pink argues, is because stories contextualize facts and provide an emotional

STORIES AS GUIDES: RESEARCH INTO HOW STORIES INFLUENCE US

Paul Zak, director of the Center for Neuroeconomic Studies, and his team of researchers found that when people listened to a sad story about a terminally ill two-year-old and his father, their brains responded by releasing two chemicals: cortisol and oxytocin. Cortisol is a chemical that focuses our attention on something important and, in this case, directly correlated with people's sense of distress after hearing the story. Oxytocin correlated with people's sense of empathy. Zak's team then asked people to donate money to a stranger or a charity after hearing the story. They found that the amount of these two chemicals released predicted how much money the people would share. Zak says, "The narrative changes behavior by changing our brain chemistry" (Casebeer and Zak 2013). The researchers found that not just any old story would elicit these same responses. When they told participants a story about a two-year-old and his father taking a daytrip to the zoo, there was no significant response. For the brain to change chemically, they found, stories must follow the dramatic arc (as first articulated by Gustav Freytag 150 years ago) of exposition, rising action, climax, falling action, and denouement.

So where does all this research lead us? To the fact that the brain seeks stories, and the stories it writes guide self-image and future behavior. Our classrooms can be sources of empowering stories for our communities of learners.

element (112). In other words, they integrate the whole brain. Daniel Pink highlights the words of Ursula K. LeGuin, the great science fiction writer: "The story—from Rumpelstiltskin to *War and Peace*—is one of the basic tools invented by the human mind for the purpose of understanding. There have been great societies that did not use the wheel, but there have been no societies that did not tell stories" (105). Rather than just telling a child, "You are optimistic," crafting a story about a time the child was optimistic will have deeper impact, last longer, and more likely influence future behavior because we are wired to respond to stories.

Using Class Shares and Meetings to Create Positive Personal Narratives

The stories that make us who we are don't necessarily need to cast us in the role of hero. Rather, we glean information about social norms and personal identity from stories all around us: TV, movies, myths, books (Perry 2009, 96–97). In fact, the stories we hear about others can influence our actions and ways of thinking. Research has found that people who watch television with a great deal of violence are more likely to believe that they will become victims of violence (Perry 2009, 101). For that reason, even when telling a story about a single child, it is helpful to tell that story to the whole class in order to create an oral anthology of sorts that says, "We are the kind of class that acts in these ways."

Class shares and community meetings provide excellent opportunities to build these storytelling structures into your day. These three- to five-minute tales can close out an activity or begin a class or morning meeting. In our experience, children move speedily to the rug when given the promise of a story, which will ease transitions and perhaps even help you find a few more minutes in your day.

Storytelling does not need to be elaborate or incorporate fancy props. As you will see in the following peek into a first-grade classroom, employing a few simple techniques to increase engagement is often all it takes to make a story memorable and have children request it again and again.

Storytelling About Success Through Persistence: Window into First Grade

The classroom is bustling with the energy of cleanup from writing. A few kids are struggling to fit their writing into their folders; a few others are hurriedly returning staplers and tape dispensers to their locations so they can find their spots with the rest of the community. Excepting these few stragglers, the rest of the class is settled in a circle on the rug. The teacher, Ms. Kat, pulls out two child-made fire logs from the easel and drops them in the center of the circle and, in a hush, begins the story.

- Playful props, such as campfire logs, a flashlight, or a pretend microphone, easily increase theatricality and make the time feel special.
- Sitting in a circle underscores the community aspect of storytelling. Children will easily be able to look between the teacher and the important players in this story.

Kat opens a make-believe book on her lap and pretends to find a certain page. She smiles as a few first graders mimic her actions. She begins, "Ahhh, here is the story I wanted to tell you!" She sweeps her fingers across the space in front of her as though gesturing to a theater marquis and says, "'The Time Ella Was Persistent'!"

At this moment all the kids swing their eyes toward Ella, who drops her head and giggles a little. "Will you help me tell it?" Kat asks, looking toward Ella, who nods. "Maybe we can all tell it," she continues.

- Keep a log of whom you tell stories about so you can make sure everyone has a chance to shine in the spotlight.
- Co-construct the story with the "stars" as much as possible to incorporate their emotional experience and right brain.

"Once upon a time, a writer named Ella was working on a book called *All About Superheroes*." Kat begins miming writing an invisible book. "She wrote and wrote until suddenly she came to a problem!" Kat makes a face of frustration and balls her fists up as though angry. "What was that problem, you ask? She wanted to spell a Very Big Word: *superheroes*!" You can hear the capital letters in Kat's voice—her emphasis on each word and the way she makes fireworks with her hands for each beat. She looks at Ella and continues, "Ella thought, 'This is a hard word; what can I do?'" Kat taps her head as though thinking, and many of the children copy her.

- Use conventional storytelling language—*once upon a time*, *and then*, *suddenly*, and so on—to model the structure of stories.
- Act out the story as you go and encourage kids to join you. This will make the story easier for children to repeat later.
- Use exact dialogue when possible.

At this moment, Kat turns to Ella and asks her, "What did you do, Ella?"

Ella fills in the blank by saying, "I tried and tried, like, a hundred times!"

Kat picks this up and weaves it into the story. "So Ella took a deep breath and said to herself, 'I can try! And if it doesn't work, I can try again!'"

At this point, Vijay shouts out, "She used persistence!"

- Using previously established self-talk (see Chapters 5 and 6) in the story can help children make the connection between an idea (e.g., use persistence) and an action (e.g., try a few times).
- Make sure you choose a story that has realistic applications for other children. Trying to spell a word a few times is likely to help a child get closer to spelling it and is good practice for all. This would not be a good technique for someone trying to read a book that was much too hard—it is not true in that case that you could try it several times and eventually it would work.

Kat continues the thread of the story. "So Ella took a deep breath and stretched it slowly out, /sooooop/, and wrote some letters; /errrrrr/, wrote some more; /hhhh/ /eaaarrrrrrr/, wrote, wrote; /ooooooosssss/. And then she looked at it and thought, 'Hmmm, not yet; let me try this again!'" At this point Kat produces Ella's book, which shows her multiple attempts at figuring out the word.

"So she stretched it again [*Kat points to the second attempt*] and again [*Kat points to the third attempt*] and again, just like Max in *Bunny Cakes*!" Kat points to the fourth and final attempt. She looks to Ella and asks, "Ella how did you know to stop?"

Ella's answer indicates some of the strategies that Kat has taught around stretching tricky words. "Well, because it had all the sounds I could hear and it looked right; it looked like how it looks in superhero books."

Kat adds this to the story, "Finally Ella stopped and looked at her word! 'I did it!' she said! 'It looks right and has all the sounds I need!' Ella kept on writing, knowing that if she found another hard word, persistence, or trying another time, just might help her!"

- Refer to fictional and historical figures your class knows well to help children make connections.
- Weave instructional support into the story, for example, "looked right and had all the sounds."
- Make your ending restate the idea you want children to hold onto; endings tend to be the most memorable parts of stories.

Kat wraps up this story, which has taken about three minutes, with this request: "Friends, can you turn and tell your neighbor a story around the campfire of a time when you used persistence and it helped you out of a tricky spot?"

- Float around and listen in. Many of these stories will sound like variations of your story, and that is OK.
- Help kids craft an ending that summarizes the experience.
- Coach into children's stories to help them better capture their self-talk.

Kat gives them a minute or two, and then claps her hands to gather the group's attention. "OK, persistent people, can you get next to your math partners on the rug so we can talk addition?"

Moving from Idea to Action

One story, told one time, does not carry nearly the same neural impact as many stories, told many times. Storytelling can feel awkward or uncomfortable for adults, and so at first we, as teachers, can sometimes let it slip away. To make the biggest impact, we have to hold ourselves to a commitment of telling stories about the children in our class daily. The next chapter will give you the tools to find the time and the tone that work for you.

Using Storytelling to Build Positive Mental Pathways

In our classrooms, we work to construct curriculum that enlists children in identifying and meeting just-right challenges, as detailed and deconstructed in Chapters 1 and 2. We ask ourselves questions like, "What is this child just beginning to try? What does this child use but still confuse?" In being able to identify what is in a child's grasp with a little effort, we are able to set up scenarios that yield stories of success. Sometimes this means offering a few strategies to help a child read the *Star Wars* book she has been cradling for a month or giving just enough information about a math problem for children to dig in with lively debate and theories. It is a guarantee that most children have scenarios in their lives that are beyond their control: poverty, divorce, fear, even little brothers or sisters that ruin block towers. That is why it is essential that we, as teachers, create a predictable environment that is under children's control. It is the ability to defeat small challenges now that will help children defeat large challenges later. In teaching children to advocate for themselves now, we can help them advocate for change later. When we tell stories of children fighting for equality on the playground, we help them join the fight for equality as adults. Storytelling can be a way to build children's esteem and sense of agency, and by telling these stories, we set the foundation for a just and democratic future.

In Your Own Classroom

You may already feel the burning desire to build more storytelling into your day, but that desire may be met just as strongly with the fear that there is just not enough time. Storytelling does not have to become something to add into your day; rather, it can be woven in across your day and can serve the curricular purposes of reinforcing strategies, establishing productive learning stances, and building a sense of story structure. The table "Integrating Storytelling Within a Daily Framework" suggests some easy ways to incorporate storytelling into your existing schedule.

Integrating Storytelling Within a Daily Framework

Time of Day	Ways to Integrate Storytelling
Morning meeting	• Open the day with a quick story of the day before. • Have children tell each other a story as you wait for them to settle in. • Put a picture up and have children tell a story about it.
Reading, writing, and math workshops	• Start the lesson with a story or by having a student share a relevant story. • Stop independent work midway through and tell a quick story of something you noticed. • Wrap up the work time with a story.
Transitions	• Tell the children gathered on the rug a story. • Spend the first few minutes back from lunch or recess with a story.
Afternoon meeting/end of day	• Look at the schedule and tell a story from one part of the day. • Have children share a story from the day. • Put up a picture or piece of work from the day and have children tell a story about it.
Anytime	• Keep a space in the room where you and your students can jot story ideas on sticky notes so you can tell them at other times.

Soon, this small daily habit (three to five minutes) will start to reap huge rewards. You will have written your own creation myths for your classroom, emphasizing certain stances, behaviors, and values. These will become guiding principles for your classroom, and your students, the way our own stories have been for us. As Philippa Perry warns us, we must be careful of our own "fears, anxieties, prejudices, and restrictive patterns of being" (2009, 96) as we select and tell stories to make sure we keep our students and their needs at the forefront. It is not that we should invent stories but that we should help children put the best possible spin on the events that occur. This may be as simple as retelling the story of a child who fell at recess as one of resilience, in which the child got back up to play, or the story of a child abandoning a too-hard book as one of flexibility, in which the child invested in just-right challenges.

We all know a good storyteller (you may even be one), but for the rest of us, telling a story can feel a little intimidating. There is no formula for telling a great story, but there are some tips that will help you moving forward:

1. Choose a real (and common) event.
2. Plan the key points before you begin and tell it sequentially.
3. Use dialogue and dramatization throughout.
4. Give children a chance to immediately retell the story or tell a related story.

REVISITING THE BLOCK SCENARIO

Think back to the block scenario from the previous chapter. Imagine that the class gathered on the rug later in the day, and the teacher said, "Friends, I have a story to tell you." And then slowly and carefully, the teacher began: "Once upon a time in this very classroom, three friends were trying to build the biggest block tower in the world. Now, these optimistic builders carefully, carefully put block on top of block until it grew even bigger than the biggest kid. Then, as one more block went up . . . *Oh no!* It came tumbling down. The builders were very sad. Some even wanted to give up! But then these three friends realized whenever you try to do something kind of risky, like building a tall block tower, it might fall down. Were they the type of kids who let that stop them? No; if they were brave enough to try it, they were brave enough to fix it! They thought and thought until they came up with the best idea of them all! They would be resilient and build it again with an even bigger bottom, so that when they got to the top, it wouldn't fall over. And guess what? It worked! These three friends learned that even when things are hard, they are bounce-back kids! They take a deep breath, think about what to try differently, and go for it!"

Choose a Real (and Common) Event

The classroom setting is rife with stories. You just have to train yourself, and your community members, to be on the lookout for them. Sometimes you may be handed a gift: a child who helps another child in a great show of empathy or a child who used to unravel after a setback now taking a water break and getting back to work. But sometimes you have to help the story along a little, and that is OK too. Oftentimes when we are working with children one-on-one or in small groups, we coach them into using productive self-talk or being flexible. These events make great stories; just leave your role out when you tell the story so it does not cast you as the great savior. As these events occur, it's helpful to jot them on stickies, or have children jot them, for later use (e.g., "Maggie—resilient at recess"). You can even dedicate a space in the classroom for these notes (see Figure 8.1).

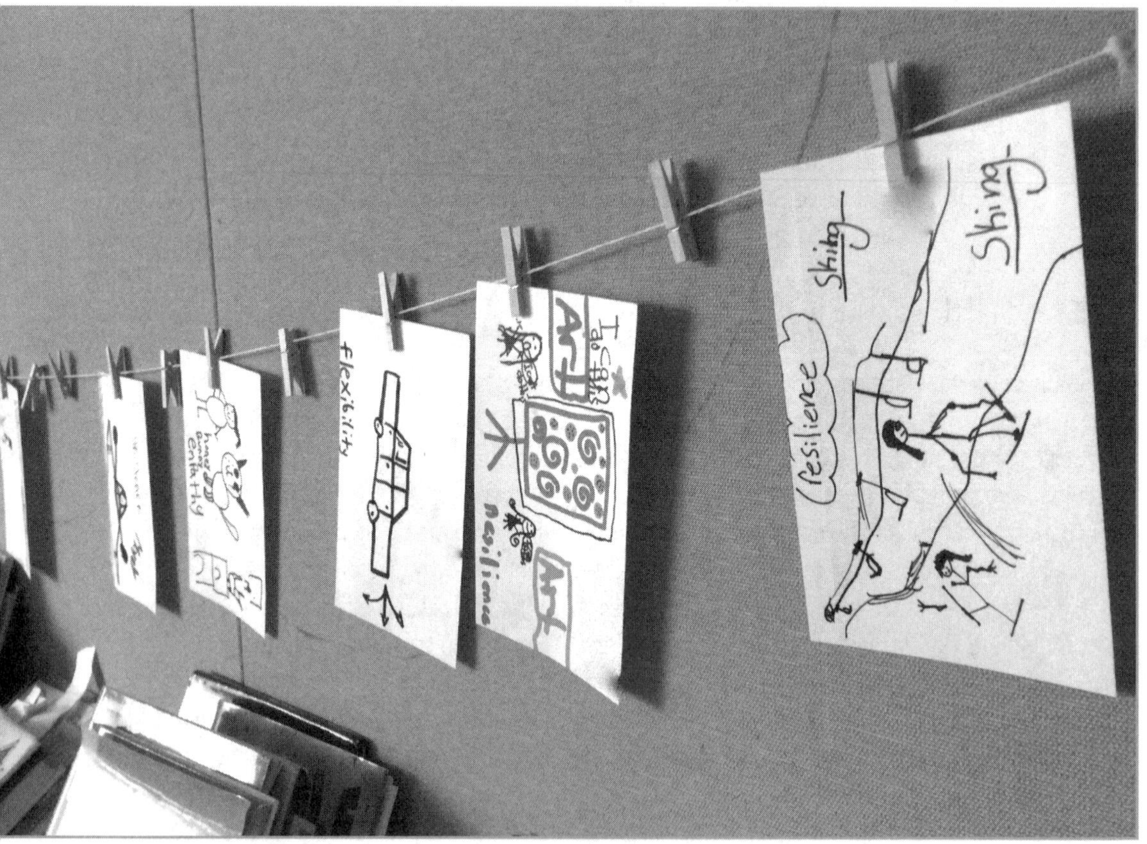

FIGURE 8.1 A Classroom Clothesline with Story Cards

When selecting a story to tell, we choose one that will be helpful for a lot of children. If you find the bulk of your class is persistent to a fault, for example, expending a lot of effort with no change in results, a story about flexibility might be in order. If you find that your children are more interested in "already knowing" something over learning it, you may find that a story about optimism and curiosity will go a long way.

When selecting a story, work hard to be realistic. Don't lie. This is harder than it sounds. If you tell a story about a child being flexible by taking her second choice in centers, don't gloss over the disappointment or make it magically all better. Be honest that the choice was hard, and it didn't feel great, but she made the second choice because she really wanted to play and knew that the next time might be different if she got to choose early. Finding the positive spin does not mean that everything becomes the best ever; rather, it means we acknowledge negative feelings and help children move past them into productive actions.

We would never, as adults, share a story of a person staying in an unhealthy, abusive work environment as a model of the power of persistence. We are mindful that we do not do that to children either. The stories we tell also honor changing course, advocating for change, and walking away. We even tell our own stories as teachers of changing the way we've been doing things because they haven't been working for our students. These stories will help children make sense of the world, and in the world there are very real and powerful times to do all those things. In Kat's classroom, she knew persistence and multiple attempts would help children get closer to conventional spelling—it is a well-tested strategy—therefore, the story she told set her children up for realistic success (see Chapter 7).

Plan Key Points and Tell the Story Sequentially

Have you ever gone into a frozen yogurt shop, the kind that lets you choose your flavors and toppings on your own, and come out with a sundae of horrors? We have, and the same kind of mishap can occur when you launch into a story with no clear plan of how it will go. Forty-five minutes later, you may still be rambling with no point (and no audience). The best tip we can offer is one as old as time but still supported by research (see the box "Stories as Guides" in Chapter 7): plan it like a story mountain.

1. Set the scene (the who and the where).
2. Name the challenge or problem.
3. Raise the tension through multiple attempts or worsening events.
4. Reach a resolution.

Looking at Kat's story, we can break it down in the following way:

1. **Scene:** Ella and writing
2. **Problem:** tricky word
3. **Tension:** she tried again and again
4. **Resolution:** she got to a point where it looked right and had all the sounds

Our caveat to this is that you will likely want to include the self-talk or stance that helped the child reach a resolution—it's not that the child magically resolved the issue but that a particular stance or action helped move the problem to resolution. There is no need to get fancy with flashbacks and time jumps; sequential order will be easier to remember and easier to tell and retell.

Use Dialogue and Dramatization Throughout

Children often remember the dialogue of stories before anything else. Kristi's two-year-old niece retells the five little monkeys story by shaking her finger and saying, "No, no bad monkeys," five times in a row. Read a favorite like *Caps for Sale*, and within seconds, children will be chiming in with, "Caps, caps for sale! Fifty cents a cap!" We can capitalize on this engaging and memory-hooking device by incorporating dialogue, especially empowering self-talk or conversation, into our own stories. Children will remember this and repeat it, which is one of our goals. In Kat's story, she used dialogue when she had Ella say, "I can try, and if it doesn't work, I can try again!" Much like the peddler's refrain in *Caps for Sale*, the repetition of this phrase will help children remember and use it.

Incorporating movement is just as essential in increasing retention. Listening to a story lights up one section of the brain, and seeing gestures lights up another. The more parts of the brain we can light up with our stories (and our teaching), the more likely children will be to remember them (Hattie and Yates 2013, 141). Don't fret; it does not have to turn into a one-man show, but a few simple actions—tapping your head, pretending to write, and so on—can make a difference. If you can, use a photograph or the student's work as well to help make your story come to life.

Give Children a Chance to Immediately Retell the Story or Tell a Related Story

Storytelling has multiple aims: to model the structure of story and the detail that makes it powerful, to transmit an idea about what is important in the classroom, to develop oral language and listening skills. Purely listening to stories has its own benefits, but when we engage children in the retelling of a story or the creation of their own stories, we awaken some sleeping parts of the brain. Children need to activate their language centers, they need to organize and sequence, and they need to work metacognitively, asking, in Kat's case, "When did persistence help me?" These stories can in turn become fuel for writing workshops, tools for understanding characters in reading, and models for behavior in future situations.

Just as we want to be sensitive about helping all children find a place in our stories, we also want to make sure we are telling diverse types of stories. One of our primary purposes for storytelling is to help each child build a tool kit of strategies for dealing with difficulty or novelty. We find it helpful to keep a list of the stances we are working on and jot the date and topic of each story we tell around them, so that we do not tell stories of resilience, for example, for three weeks straight (see Figure 8.2).

We can overwork one muscle group only to find that we don't have the strength to carry the groceries home. Likewise, persistence is not the best tool for a multitude of situations.

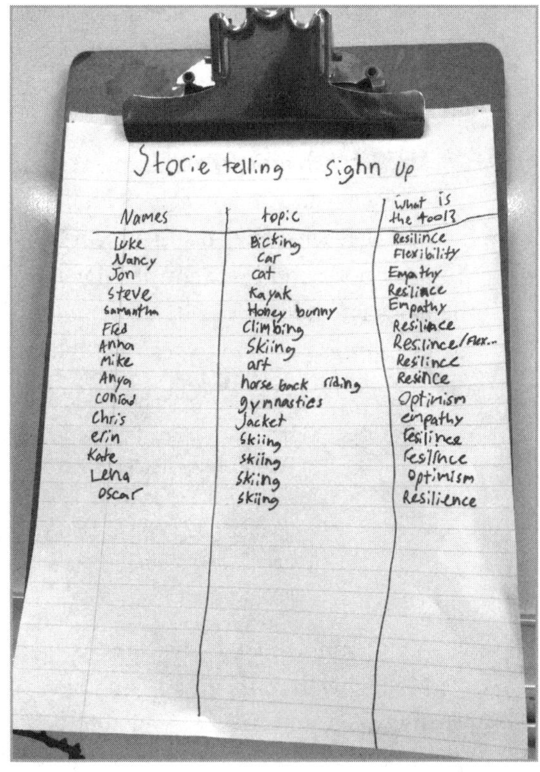

FIGURE 8.2 Clipboard for Record Keeping: Names and Topics

As soon as you have told one story, the stage is ready to be shared. We often coach children as they lead the story, helping them to make their story as clear and powerful as possible. Sometimes we will just have children tell a story to their neighbor of a time they helped change something for the better or displayed empathy. There is no set model for who needs to tell the story, or when the story must be told, only that stories stick with us and their value in helping shape identity and actions cannot be overstated.

In the following example, Ms. Schwab turns the storytelling reins over to one of her fifth-grade students, Jack. These students have spent the first few weeks of the school year thinking and talking about the power and necessity of optimism in their learning. They have heard story after story of classroom and real-life examples of risk taking. By allowing Jack to take the spotlight, Ms. Schwab is starting to lift the scaffolding and transfer the ownership of this lifelong skill to her students.

Student-Led Storytelling: Window into Fifth Grade

Stories from the weekend buzz around the classroom as Ms. Schwab quickly takes attendance and fills out a lunch count. It is Monday morning and her students call out to each other from across the classroom as they unstack chairs and slowly make their way to the meeting area.

Ms. Schwab overhears Jack telling of his "epic" hike up Mount Washington, the highest peak in the northeast: "When I first saw it, I didn't think I could make it. But then I decided that it didn't hurt to give it a shot. And it was so sweet at the top."

- Monday mornings—as hectic as they are—are ripe for storytelling, especially with older students, who love to live and relive the stories of their weekends.
- Think about how stories can be framed, but keep them authentic and real.

Ms. Schwab quickly walks over to Jack. "Hey, Jack. Do you think you could tell that story at morning meeting? I'd like to hear the whole thing and it seems like it fits perfectly with our optimism work."

Jack nods and Ms. Schwab suggests, "Why don't you grab Clare, head out into the hallway, and practice it. You could make a quick story arc and try to remember the key things you said to yourself that were really motivating."

- Focus the story on the quality that you would like to highlight—in this case, optimism. Later, this story could be retold through a different lens to highlight another quality, such as persistence or flexibility, but the angle of the story would change.
- Just as you need to plan your stories, students need to plan and practice. Giving them a chance to rehearse will increase their confidence and improve their story.

A few minutes later, the class has settled down into a circle on the rug.

Ms. Schwab pulls an antique book off the marker rail, blows fictitious dust off the cover, and opens to a page. "Fifth graders, it is with great pleasure that I announce that today's tale of optimism and daring comes to you from our very own Jack."

Ms. Schwab gets up from her rocking chair, carefully hands the book over to Jack, and takes a spot on the rug next to him.

- Rituals and props can go a long way with older students, too, and once they're established, they draw the class' attention to the storyteller.
- When a student is storytelling, make sure you remain very close to whisper coaching tips to him without disrupting the momentum of the story (see "Lifting the Level of Storytelling over Time" later in this chapter for more coaching tips).

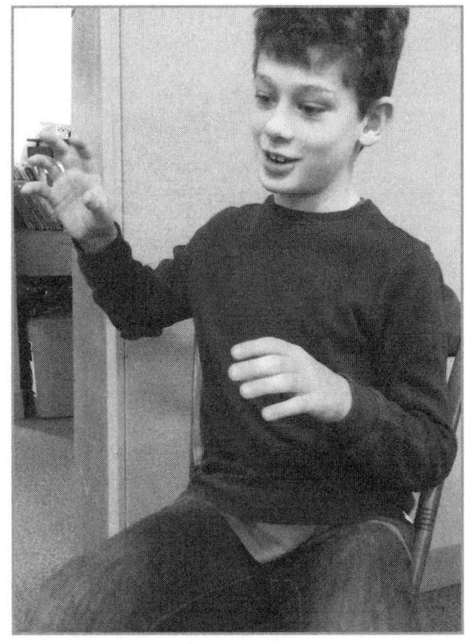

FIGURE 8.3 Jack Telling His Story of Optimism

Jack settles into the chair, holds the book on his lap, and gives a small smirk. "On Saturday I went with my family . . . ," Jack starts.

"It's such a great story," whispers Ms. Schwab kindly. "Tell it like the great story that it is."

Jack restarts: "Early one morning, not so far from here, I woke up with a start." Ms. Schwab smiles and nods.

"It was a day that I had been dreading for weeks."

Ms. Schwab leans in to whisper, "Show us what dread looks like?" as a cue to add gestures. Jack shakes his head slowly from side to side as though in denial that this day has come to pass.

- Make sure the storyteller begins with the right tone; it can carry the whole story.
- Coach into both the words and the dramatization of the story. Model or cue for hand gestures and facial changes.

"The day my family had picked to hike *Mount Washington*." At this, Jack throws up his arms and gazes upward, and his classmates follow his gaze and groan softly.

"In the car, at first, I was like, 'I do not want to do this.'" Jack shakes his head and crosses his arms. "And then when we got closer, my dad pointed to this huge mountain in the distance." Jack throws up his arms again. "Then I thought, 'I *can't* do that!'"

Jack pauses for effect and glances around the circle at his classmates. They are hooked.

"We got out of the car at the trailhead, and I was moving so slowly. I kept thinking, 'I can't.' But then," Jack continues, snapping his fingers, "something changed."

"How did it change? Be specific!" Ms. Schwab whispers.

"All of a sudden, I remembered those lines from *The Magician's Elephant* that we've been saying over and over again. 'What if? Why not? Could it be?'" Jack paused. "I asked myself, 'What if I hiked to the top? Why not give it a try? Could I really make it?'" (See Figure 8.4.)

- As a student gets to the heart of a story, make sure he is prepared to name the key phrase that will be relatable and replicable for the whole class. You may want to have the student jot it down on a sticky note beforehand and keep it with him as he tells his story.

The magicians elephant
INQUIRY
INTO
Optimism
What if? Why not? Could it be?
• Is his sister alive?
• Peter makes the choice to believe.
• Sometimes optimism is hard.
• Sometimes the people all around you can make you more optimistic.
• Unexpected things can make a difference.

FIGURE 8.4 Chart from *The Magician's Elephant* Inquiry into Optimism

Jack looks around the circle. "So I pulled the laces on my boots tight, I looked up at the mountain, and I said to my dad, 'I'm ready.' And do you know what?" Jack asks in a whisper. "Every time I started to think that the mountain was too big, I would just think, 'What if?'"

"What if . . . *what*?" Ms. Schwab whispers with raised eyebrows, shrugged shoulders, and open palms.

"I would think to myself, 'What if I tried just a little bit harder and went just a little bit farther?' and before I knew it, I was at the top of the mountain. At the top of the tallest mountain in the northeast!" Jack beams.

"What did it take to get there?" Ms. Schwab nudges.

"All it took to get there was a little optimism. . . . And," Jack says, smiling, "a couple of granola bars, two water bottles, and a turkey sandwich."

The class laughs and Ms. Schwab leads the audience in a round of applause.

- Once the quality you are studying is "in the water," students will be able to name it and see its connection to a multitude of stories. If a story ends before they get a chance to do so, nudge the storyteller in that direction.
- Having a class chart near the meeting area that displays the constellation of qualities can serve as a reminder to all storytellers—including you!—to bring stories to a close with an important, transferrable message.

"Fifth graders," she says to pull them back together. "If I were going to guess, I'd say lots of you have stories just like Jack's about how you used optimism this weekend and maybe you even asked, 'What if?' Let's think now about how Jack's story could help us as learners. How can we use this story to kick-start our week? Turn and talk to someone near you."

- When students tell stories from their lives outside of school, you can take a moment to have them relate the stories to their learning and lives in school. Highlighting the transferability of these qualities will prove just how authentic this work is and will be for their whole lives.
- Later in the week, or later in the day, you may want to follow up a story like Jack's with a story of optimism that took place right inside the classroom.

Ms. Schwab circles around, listening in to the conversations for a few minutes, and then rings a chime. She quickly wraps up by restating one or two ideas from the partnerships and then transitions. "All right, fifth graders, let's take a look at our schedule. What's next?"

LIFTING THE LEVEL OF STORYTELLING OVER TIME

Taking the time to tell stories helps cement story structure in a child's mind. By modeling well-crafted stories and coaching children as they tell their own, you are also building skills they will need in writing and reading. Marie Clay has written extensively on the connections that exist between oral language, reading, and writing (2014, 122).

The Common Core State Standards identify narrative as one of the three types of writing one has to become proficient at to be "college and career ready." Whatever you spend time on, you will get better at, providing you work on it constantly. As children tell stories, listen for the structure (beginning, middle, end), the selection and quality of details (talking, action, feelings), and the rising and falling tension. Coaching into these first in oral storytelling times is a low-stress way to build habits that will find their way into children's writing. Thinking across storytelling for the year, when you listen to children's narratives, you may first concern yourself with structure, then details, then the use of mood and tension. The table "Supporting Storytelling Through Questioning" provides a few questions you might ask yourself, or your children, when telling a story to lift the level of the narrative.

SUPPORTING STORYTELLING THROUGH QUESTIONING

Story Elements	Coaching Questions
Beginnings, setting the scene	• What happened first? • Who was there? • What did you see around you? Use your five senses. • Can you think of another way to begin—talking, action? • What story words could start this? *Once upon a time . . . ; one dark, stormy night . . .* ?
Building tension	• What did the character say? Do? • Act it out—what actions go with that feeling? • Make your voice match the mood. How does this part feel? How will it sound?
Endings	• Can you say the big idea? • What happened last? • Can you end another way—talking, action, feeling?

As children become more proficient in oral storytelling, the same questions can lift the level of written (or drawn) stories during independent writing times.

Reflecting on and Maintaining Growth

In his book *The Storytelling Animal*, science writer Jonathan Gottschall writes,

> An average daydream is about fourteen seconds long and . . . we have about two thousand of them per day. In other words, we spend about half of our waking hours—one-third of our lives on earth—spinning fantasies. We daydream about the past: things we should have said or done, working through our victories and failures. We daydream about mundane stuff such as imagining different ways of handling conflict at work. But we also daydream in a much more intense, story-like way. We screen films with happy endings in our minds, where all our wishes—vain, aggressive, dirty—come true. And we screen little horror films, too, in which our worst fears are realized. (2013, 11)

As educators, our goal is for our students to use these thousands of daily moments to frame and reframe their lives in a positive, energizing way. As they gain independence in telling stories, our work shifts from supporting and coaching stories to guiding students to tell stories on their own, in the exact moment when a story of optimism or resilience, flexibility or persistence will carry them forward. The challenge becomes, then, shifting storytelling from intentional practice to simply habit.

Charles Duhigg, in his book *The Power of Habit*, describes what he calls the "Habit Loop" (2014, 19). This process consists of three steps. First, a cue (a time of day, a certain place, a smell) tells your brain which habit to use. Next, you engage in a physical, mental, or emotional routine. Finally, the reward tells your brain if this loop is worth retaining. The brain, according to Duhigg, craves these habitual loops only if they end in a positive reward. These cravings can have both positive and negative effects on our behavior. In graduate school, Christine found that a craving for distraction from writing a term paper, for example, was cued by the "ding" of an incoming message on her phone, followed by the routine of reading that message and the reward of hearing from a friend and—let's face it—not doing her work. By simply disabling the cue (or burying her phone under a pile of books), she found her mind did not crave the same reward and she was much more focused on her work.

On the other hand, the habit loop can be used to our advantage. If you would like something to become a habit, such as going running in the morning, Duhigg explains, it's important that you choose a simple cue (such as leaving your running clothes next to your bed) and a simple reward (the release of endorphins or sense of accomplishment). But just rewarding your routine will not be enough; your brain also needs to "expect the reward, to crave the endorphins or the sense of accomplishment" (2014, 51). The cue, Duhigg argues, must trigger not just the routine but also the reward to come.

In the case of storytelling, students can be coached on the times (the cues) that indicate when a story (the routine) would be especially helpful (the reward). Eventually, their brains will learn to crave these stories and use them at the first sign of stress or trouble. We find stories to be especially helpful to warm up to a challenge, to rebound from a failure or stuck point, and to cool down and reflect on an experience, reexamining it in a positive, productive way.

Check in Regularly with the Ecosystem of the Classroom

To help children become habitual storytellers, we recommend spending time as a whole class practicing which cues or triggers in our day-to-day lives indicate that a story might be especially helpful.

- **Chart:** Make a list of the times when a story would be helpful and the questions that can guide students to the right story (see the table "Building Storytelling Habits"). Have students tally or jot notes on stickies when they use the chart and celebrate these moments of practice.
- **Role-Play:** Acting out stories from the classroom can provide students with additional examples to refer to and help create a culture of storytelling. Have students explain a tricky situation and then have others tell or act out a story that could help.
- **Reflect:** Talk about times when storytelling worked especially well, and keep a record of the feelings (accomplishment, confidence, joy) that followed as the rewards.

Check in Regularly with Individual Storytelling

Just as with any skill, some students will need more coaching and practice to gain independence. For those students, we recommend several scaffolds to help them develop this habit.

- **Sketches of key images from a story,** on sticky notes, placed where a student might need them most, can serve as visual cues to tell a particular story at a particular time.
- **Photographs or mementos** placed nearby a child can be quick reminders of a story of success.

Building Storytelling Habits

Cues (When a Story Might Be Needed)	Routines (Questions to Elicit a Helpful Story)
To warm up	• Is there a story of optimism or risk that can help me get started? • What will the story be if I give this a shot?
To rebound	• Is there a story that I know about bouncing back? • What's the story of what has happened so far? How can I change that story? • What story am I telling myself right now? How is that different from what is really happening? • How can I change the story that I'm telling myself?
To cool down	• How can I tell the story of that experience? • How else could it go? • Can I put a positive spin on that story?

- **Tallies or charts** make students aware of how often they're using this skill. Individual students can tally or keep track of the number of times they used a story in a day. Alternatively, you could have students put their names on sticky notes and add them to a class chart celebrating this powerful skill.

It is our responsibility as educators to think both of the children in front of us and of the adults we hope they become. When we tell stories of children who protest for change, we create space in children's minds to believe that change is possible. When we tell stories about flexibility, we underscore that single-minded doggedness is not always as effective as a simple change of tactic. We are not storytelling just so that children can build better block structures; we are storytelling so children can build a better world.

SUGGESTIONS FOR ENGAGING FAMILIES

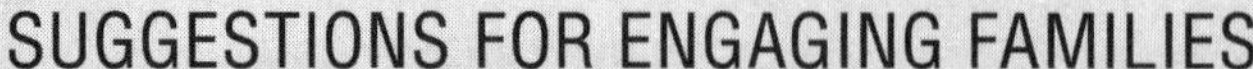

Tony Schwartz, in his article "Developing Mastery Through Deliberate Practice" (2013), speaks to the power of ritual. He writes, "A ritual is a highly precise behavior that you do at a specific time so that it becomes automatic over time and no longer requires much conscious intention or energy" (87). He goes on to say that when something becomes a ritual, you can place your energy in the important aspects of work.

Oftentimes we hear from parents, "When I ask my child what happened in school today, she says nothing!" A ritual of storytelling addresses this issue by providing every child with at least one anecdote she can tell to a caregiver. To that end, we suggest building a ritual for storytelling at home. Have parents pick a time when it will happen every day, rain or shine. Making the time and the routine consistent means that the entirety of effort can be spent lifting the quality of stories and the meaning families derive from them.

This practice is made even more powerful when you can clue the parents in to the story. Tweets, emails, even simple "Ask me about . . ." notes can connect parents intimately to the classroom. On the flip side, encouraging parents to tell stories to their children, and to co-construct stories at home, if they do not do so already, strengthens home and school connections and the bond between the members of the community.

- Encourage families to send in photos of children acting in empathetic (or resilient, flexible, etc.) ways. Children can use these pictures as springboards into oral or written stories.
- Hold a storytelling workshop for families, or invite storytellers to come in for families to enjoy, to communicate the essentials of a good story.
- Encourage families to use photo albums, mementos, and videos as sources of stories for their children.
- Send home a storytelling log, where parents and children can record the stories they tell and whom they tell them to.

Goals: Creating Just-Right Goals to Drive Growth

We have goals in all areas of our lives: exercise goals, diet goals, professional goals, personal goals, goals for the day, the week, the month, the year, and our lifetime. Some of our goals might be easy to measure. We might say, for example, "I will run a half marathon in October." But sometimes our goals are less tangible: we might set a goal to be more grateful about the good things in our life, or happier in our job, or more patient with our children. Goals can leave us shouting from the rooftops with an unmatched sense of joy and accomplishment. They can drive us to be courageous, consistent, and mindful. But goals can also leave us dragging ourselves—literally or figuratively—across a finish line. Mention New Year's resolutions to a group of friends in February, and groans will surely ensue. At times, goals feel as though they just serve to highlight our mistakes and failures. Why is this the case? Why do some goals motivate us to change our habits and our lives and others leave us exactly where we started? And when we are working with the children in our classes, how can we use goals to leverage their engagement, motivation, and use of the constellation of stances?

There was a general store down the road from Christine's childhood home that made the Best Chocolate Chip Cookies in the Universe. When Christine was ten, she set a goal to replicate these cookies. The goal was lofty, but the motivation was clear: delicious chocolate chip cookies at her disposal at any time. Several spectacular failures later (the first due to the interpretation of "soda" as root beer rather than baking soda), Christine was just a hair closer to the coveted cookies. Looking over the most recent batch of rock-solid disks, her mom noted, "Well, these *taste* closer to what you're going for. I wonder how you could make them softer and chewier?" And with that, the experimenting continued until Christine discovered just the exact moment to take her cookies out of the oven. Did she ever match the Best Chocolate Chip Cookies in the Universe? No. But that's the thing about goals: even when they're impossible to meet, they get us just far enough down a path that we find ourselves launched into our next goal. For Christine, this just so happened to be chocolate cake.

Goals can have a powerful impact on how we live our lives. They require us to engage the entire constellation of stances as we set and work toward a specific outcome. Yet perhaps most importantly, they provide our students with an opportunity to develop their own agency and identity in our classrooms.

Leveraging Engagement and Motivation with Meaningful Goals

Sometimes for teachers, it can feel as though it is a tale of two worlds in one classroom. At times, our students jump up from a minilesson and race over to their writing or math or reading, unable to contain their excitement and emitting audible groans when we call them back together. At other times, the minutes in a lesson seem to tick by extraordinarily slowly, for us and our students. It seems that every year another round of books, programs, and hot tips claim to have the answers to the challenging question of student motivation. These answers range from candy and stickers to class rewards like pajama day and extra recess. Sometimes these systems seem both necessary and effective. But think about a time when both teaching and learning were almost magical in your classroom, when you looked around and thought to yourself, "Ahh, this. This is what real engagement looks like." What was behind *those* moments?

True Motivation: Autonomy, Purpose, Mastery

In recent years, research has started to paint a clearer picture of what truly motivates us to learn, to challenge ourselves, or to meet our goals. Originally, motivation was thought to be either biological ("I'm thirsty; I should drink water.") or related to punishments and rewards ("If I don't recite my times tables perfectly, then I will have to miss recess to practice.") (Pink 2009, 3). However, a third motivation, a more intrinsic motivation, is what is really behind, as Daniel Pink calls it, our "drive" to learn, to accomplish challenging tasks, and to meet our goals. Daniel Pink's excellent book *Drive* (2009) maps out this third, intrinsic motivation—the motivation that should be central to our work with children.

"Rewards," according to Pink, "can deliver a short-term boost—just as a jolt of caffeine can keep you cranking for a few more hours. But the effect wears off—and worse, can reduce a person's longer-term motivation to continue the project" (8). Don't get us wrong, we love the way caffeine works. Especially on those dark, dark school mornings or when we're trying to finish a chapter of writing. Similarly, rewards can seem like the perfect, easy fix when you're grocery shopping with your kids, trying to teach your class expected behaviors, or just trying to get yourself to go the gym after work. But rewards, like caffeine, are a crutch that masks a deeper need—a need for involvement in an engaging, meaningful task. You're probably well aware that this trend is on the rise in our schools: "[Schools] are hauling out a wagon full of 'if-then' rewards—pizza for reading books, iPods for showing up to class, cash for good test scores. We're bribing students into compliance instead of challenging them into engagement" (Pink 2009, 185). In reality, these rewards-based systems are just creating a quick fix to deeper issues, and just as importantly, they are not the most effective form of motivation.

In fact, a recent study by Aubrey Alvarez and Amy Booth at Northwestern University found that preschoolers were less likely to complete a mundane pegboard task when they were rewarded with stickers than when they were offered the opportunity to learn something new. Alvarez and Booth wrote, "[This study] reinforces long-standing views of children as hungry to acquire causally rich information and tentatively suggests a new approach to rewarding young children that has the potential to encourage (rather than detract from) a mindset that embraces the pleasure and challenges of learning" (2014, 789–90).

Rather than rely on rewards (or punishments) to motivate ourselves and our students, Pink suggests we will see true motivation, true drive, if we create goals with our students that allow them to have autonomy, purpose, and mastery in their learning. The first component of this drive, autonomy, is achieved when an individual has some element of control over what he does, when he does it, whom he does it with, and how he does it (2009, 222). In Christine's cookie example, she had nearly complete autonomy: she decided what to bake, how often to try it, when to ask for help, and when to try a different recipe.

Intrinsic drive is amped up yet again when someone feels a real sense of purpose in what she is doing, when she feels that what she is doing is a part of something bigger than herself. Finally, this intrinsic drive relies on the understanding that one's efforts are not in vain—that the more the person commits to the work, the better and the closer to mastery she'll get (Pink 2009, 223).

Perhaps the most important outcome of these three components is what Mihaly Csikszentmihalyi, a professor of psychology, describes as "flow." Flow occurs when you're so engaged in working toward your goal that the activity becomes its own reward. Pink writes:

> In flow, goals are clear. You have to reach the top of the mountain, hit the ball across the net, or mold the clay just right. Feedback is immediate. The mountaintop gets closer or farther, the ball sails in or out of bounds, the pot you're throwing comes out smooth or uneven. . . . In flow, people lived so deeply in the moment, and felt so utterly in control, that their sense of time, place, and even self melted away. They were autonomous, of course. But more than that, they were engaged. They were, as poet W. H. Auden wrote, "Forgetting themselves in a function." (2009, 113)

Perhaps you've found yourself in this state of flow when you've been playing a sport (skiing, swimming, dancing, or running) or when you've engaged in creative pursuits (drawing, knitting, cooking, or gardening) or when you've been completely engrossed in your work (planning a complicated lesson, teaching an effective small group, or reading a favorite book aloud). It's this very flow that we see when we look around our classrooms and notice when our class is completely engaged. Our challenge, then, as teachers is to help our students set goals that allow them to be autonomous learners, working toward mastery in a state of flow.

Small Steps Lead to Big Changes

Think of a time where you were working toward a goal and found yourself in Csikszentmihalyi's state of flow. Maybe you were trying a new recipe or working on a piece of music or perfecting your tennis serve. What made that experience particularly rewarding? How did you use a goal—either implicitly or explicitly—to launch you into that state of flow? In the state of flow, we set a meaningful goal, we work toward it, we receive feedback, and then we set a new goal.

The most effective goals do not require large leaps but rather small steps. You'll have a better chance of running a half marathon in October if you set a goal to run three miles in June, five miles in August, and then ten miles in September. When we set a goal, the smaller the gap between what we can do and what we want to do, the more likely we are to meet that goal and then begin our work toward another. When it comes to knowledge gaps, the most effective goals are those that are bridgeable. In *Visible Learning*, Hattie and Yates write, "We will seek out and pay attention to things we already know about in an effort to increase our personal knowledge base. But we do so provided the knowledge gap itself is perceived as bridgeable within the short term. . . . We strive to close worthwhile gaps, not chasms" (2013, 6).

As we try to span a gap, the work or practice we do has a significant impact on how likely we are to make growth and achieve our goal. Perhaps you've heard of the 10,000-hour rule, a theory proposed by Anders Ericsson, a professor of psychology, that if you practice something in any field for 10,000 hours, you will be successful. While there is certainly validity in the idea that a goal requires a fair amount of practice, it is the *kind* of practice that is important, not just the amount.

Hattie and Yates describe how deliberate, goal-directed practice is key to growth: "Performers are presented with tasks initially outside of current performance levels, but which can be mastered within hours by focusing on critical aspects and refining technique through repetition and feedback" (2013, 96).

The feedback of a friend, a coach, or a colleague given at just the right moment can propel you toward your goal. "Receiving appropriate feedback," according to Hattie and Yates, "is incredibly empowering. Why? Because it enables the individual to move forward, to plot, plan, adjust, rethink, and thus exercise self-regulation in realistic and balanced ways. This mental processing view of feedback brings with it an important caveat. Feedback works because the goal is known and accurately defined through realistic assessment" (2013, 66). (See the following box for more on the principles of effective feedback.)

Athletes, artists, and authors alike know that no matter how hard you work toward something, it is impossible to reach true mastery. In *Drive*, Daniel Pink writes, "The joy is in the pursuit more than the realization" (2009, 125). For this reason, more often than not, when we reach a small goal, when we bridge a small gap, we set another goal. This goal cycle (set, practice, get feedback, revise) allows us to get a just a little closer to mastery.

As teachers, we keep each child's bridgeable goals and the child's work toward mastery in our minds simultaneously. We think about what can propel students forward today and what kinds of writers, mathematicians, thinkers, and people we want them to be in twenty years. As we turn our attention to our work in the classroom, you will see that we can use goals to maximize not only our students' academic growth but also their use of the constellation of stances.

JOHN HATTIE AND MARK GAN'S PRINCIPLES OF EFFECTIVE FEEDBACK

- "It is important to focus on how feedback is received rather than how it is given" (Hattie and Yates 2009, 70). Think about what kind of feedback will be most effective for the student you are working with and make sure that the student understands what you're saying. You may want him to try out what you are teaching or rephrase the feedback in his own words.
- "Feedback becomes powerful when it renders criteria for success in achieving learning goals transparent to the learner" (70). When you're giving feedback, be sure that the student understands the ultimate purpose of her goal and what it will look like when she has met that goal.
- "Feedback becomes powerful when it cues a learner's attention onto the task, and effective task-related strategies, but away from self-focus" (70). Make sure your feedback addresses *how* a goal will be met and the steps the student can take to make progress.
- "Feedback should challenge the learner to invest effort in setting challenging goals" (70). Give feedback in a manner that allows your student to be involved in his own goal setting and leaves him both excited and prepared to tackle what's next.

Pairing Optimism and Resilience in Writing: Window into Third Grade

It's early November and Ms. Kelly is glancing through several of her students' writing notebooks while they are outside at recess. The class has just started a unit on informational writing. As she reads her students' work, Ms. Kelly jots notes down on a recording form and quickly identifies a few small groups that she'll run to target specific skills.

She pauses as she opens Graham's notebook. Graham has only a few lines written on each page of his notebook. At this point in the third grade, Graham's volume of writing raises a red flag. Ms. Kelly thinks about all she knows about Graham: he's a prolific oral storyteller and is always putting on a show and trying to crack up whomever he is near. He loves reading both fiction and nonfiction, he is a strong math student but often struggles to show his work on paper, and he passionate about football, Minecraft, and skiing. Ms. Kelly also knows that despite his playful nature, Graham has a hard time recovering from setbacks and is really rather sensitive. As she mulls all of this information in her mind, Ms. Kelly adds Graham's name to her conference schedule for the afternoon and picks up another notebook.

- Before you meet with a child to set a goal, have a sense of where he is along a developmental continuum. Study his work and *how* he works.
- Don't just think of a student's work in a single subject in isolation; think of what you know about the *whole* child. (For more on observation, see Chapter 2 and Appendices C and D.)

Later that afternoon during writing, Ms. Kelly grabs her notes and slides a chair over to Graham's side. She smiles and says, "How's it going?"

Graham shrugs and leans back in his chair. Ms. Kelly notices that Graham's mood today seems a bit deflated.

Ms. Kelly smiles and asks, "Can you talk me through what you're writing about?"

Graham sits up a little straighter. "Well," he says, "I'm writing about football."

"Ahh," Ms. Kelly says. "I know you love football. Are you just bursting at the seams to teach someone about it?"

"Yeah. I mean, I know Brandon plays soccer, but I want to teach him about football so maybe he'll switch."

"Aha!" Ms. Kelly smiles. "You have a really strong reason to write this book. The ultimate writing challenge: teaching and convincing at the same time. I wonder if it will work. . . ." The two of them glance over at Brandon with raised eyebrows. Brandon looks up, smiles, shakes his head, and bends back into his writing.

- The conversational element of a conference can produce some of the most valuable information for the teacher and can reveal so much more than is written on the page.
- As you meet with your student, check to see if she has autonomy, a purpose for what she is doing, and a desire to work toward mastery. If one of these components is even just slightly off, any goal you set could fall flat.

"So what's going well for you with your writing?" Ms. Kelly asks.

"Well, I have lots of chapters about different things." Graham flips through his pages. "Positions, plays, teams, equipment, safety tips, how to throw, and the most exciting parts of the game."

"I can see that," Ms. Kelly responds. "Can we read through some of your chapters?" They read the chapters. Each has just a sentence or two. (See Figure 9.1.)

"You have quite the plan for this book, Graham. You should be proud of how you've figured out what chapters to put in. Getting yourself organized that way can be pretty tricky." Ms. Kelly pauses for a moment to let the compliment settle. "So if your *ultimate* goal is to convince Brandon to make the big switch, what smaller goal do you think could help your writing get you there?"

Graham flips through his writing and shrugs.

Ms. Kelly pauses for a moment and tries a different approach: "Imagine you've finished this book and you're ready to hand it off to Brandon. What does the book look like now? What do you see on its pages?" Ms. Kelly asks.

Brandon's eyes widen. "I think it'll be kinda like one of those *Sports Illustrated* sports books with pictures and diagrams and lots of cool things about football."

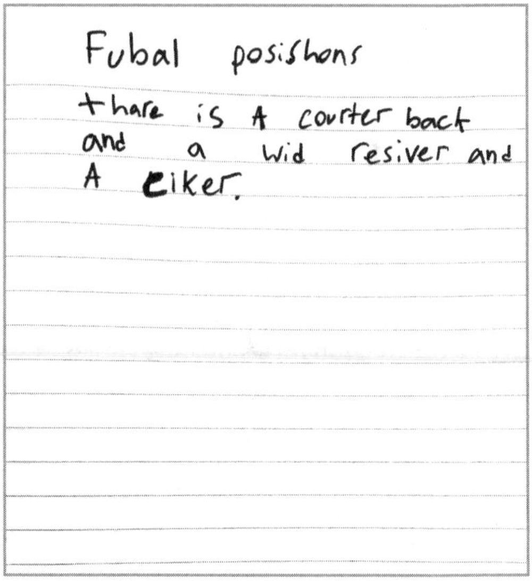

Fubal posishons

thare is A courter back and a wid resiver and A eiker.

FIGURE 9.1 Graham's "Positions" Chapter

"Oh, yeah. I can see that," Ms. Kelly replies.

- As in all conferences, be sure to compliment the child on something he is doing well and the effort that it took to get there. (For more on great resources on conferring, see Appendix A.)
- Visualizing a final product and keeping its purpose in mind can reengage students with the "why" of the work and highlight their autonomy in the process.

Ms. Kelly continues, "So, take a second to picture your future book in your mind. Can you see it? What are on its pages?" She pauses. "Now think about this: how can you get there?"

Graham taps his pen on the table. "Write a lot?" Graham asks, trying to anticipate the response he thinks Ms. Kelly is looking for.

"Is that tricky for you sometimes?" Ms. Kelly asks gently.

"Yeah," Graham responds.

"You know what, Graham? I'm going to let you in on a little secret. All writers think it's tricky to write sometimes. We all come to moments where we feel like we've run out of things to say."

"Really?" Graham asks, sounding slightly unsure.

"Really! You know what? There's even a name for it: writer's block. The most famous writers in the world struggle with what to do when they hit a wall. I wonder if there are any stances that can help with this? Let's pull out your Constellation Man and take a look." (See Figure 9.2.)

- Many of the roadblocks that students experience in learning closely mirror those that we experience in "real life." Acknowledging this can help take away those gloom-and-doom feelings and refocus students' energy on their growth.
- Ms. Kelly is working with the theory that Graham knows enough about text features and elaboration to add more to each chapter and just requires an extra boost to do so. Her work with another student, though, might focus more on specific strategies for elaboration.
- "Constellation Man" refers to a figure the class made earlier in the year. For more ideas on integrating the constellation of stances, see Chapters 3 and 4.

Graham and Ms. Kelly study each stance on Constellation Man and decide that a combination of optimism and resiliency might be most helpful.

"OK. So you're going to work on developing your optimism and resiliency when you run into writer's block. What if you set this goal: 'When I run out of things to say and hit a wall, I'll develop my resiliency and optimism and think, "I can do this! What else do I need to teach Brandon? How can I teach that information?"' What do you think?"

"Yeah! I like that."

"Excellent! Draw up a sticky note reminder and then we'll give it a try."

Graham draws a quick reminder of the goal, including the wall, the class symbols for optimism and resilience, a sketch of his buddy Brandon, and a tiny book with an *I* on it for information (see Figure 9.3). While he is doing this, Ms. Kelly jots Graham's goal and a few notes down on her conferring sheet (see Figure 9.4).

FIGURE 9.2 Constellation Man

FIGURE 9.3 Graham's Sticky Note Reminder

FIGURE 9.4 Ms. Kelly's Conferring Notes

Ms. Kelly - Writing Workshop - Conferring Notes - 2014-2015

Date/Name	Child says	Observations /Teaching	Goal
Graham 11.4.14	· convincing B to play football · lots of chapters about diff things · "write a lot" ↑ tricky	· VOLUME!! · he knows a lot re: football, needs to get it down · good purpose	WHEN hits a wall: Think: "I can do this" "What else can I teach B? How?"

- Have the child create a system for remembering her goal. This will help her internalize it and make it her own. See the following chapter for more on these reminders, or "mediators," as Vygotsky called them.
- Make sure you take time to jot down your own notes during or immediately after the conference, when the interaction is fresh in your mind.
- To help maintain motivation, keep the purpose of the task (in this case, Graham's writing) embedded within the goal.

Ms. Kelly notices that Graham is finishing up his sketch and she says, "All right, ready to give it a go?"

Graham holds up his sticky note and responds: "Yep."

"Pretend you are working on your 'Positions' chapter and—*kabam!*—you hit a wall. What do you do?"

Graham uncaps his pen and pretends to write across his page. "Screeech! *Pow*!" Graham shoots his hands out as he "hits a wall" and then crumples onto his desk.

"Uh-oh!" Ms. Kelly plays along.

"Dun, dun, dunnnnn," Graham says, really getting into the role-play.

- Goal-setting conferences provide the perfect opportunity for students to role-play what to do when something doesn't go quite right, and you'll find that with a little encouragement, most will happily take on this playful stance.

Graham picks up the sticky note with a flourish. "Step one," he begins, naming the steps across his fingers, "Think to myself, 'I've hit a wall, but I can get over it!' Step two: Get up." Graham gives Ms. Kelly a sideways glance to see if she caught his improv; she did and gives him a thumbs-up and gestures for him to keep going.

"Step three: Think about what I need to teach Brandon to make him want to switch to football. Step four: Think about how I can do it. Step five: Do it!"

"Graham!" Ms. Kelly says, genuinely impressed. "You nailed it. But let's go back to step four for a second. If you're working on your 'Positions' chapter, what could you add in to teach Brandon?"

Graham furrows his brow, taps his pen, and says: "I could probably add more about how defense and offense are different. Maybe I could make a diagram about where different players start a play. Or who gets to do the most tackling." Graham raises his eyebrows and smiles as he adds this last idea.

- The more your students use goals, the more they will become accustomed to telling the steps or the story of a goal in their own voice.

Ms. Kelly nods. "Well, I can see you have your work cut out for you. If I know anything about Brandon, I can tell you that this will be no easy task. He's a *big* soccer player. Are you up for the challenge?"

"Oh yeah," Graham says confidently.

Moving from Idea to Action

Some people might argue that Graham lacked stamina in writing. But stamina is a result of engaged learning, the way that falling leaves are a result of the changing seasons. You cannot force the leaves to fall and the seasons to change, just as you cannot force stamina and get engagement. To that end, stamina is not a goal; engagement in learning is. Ms. Kelly used a goal to reengage Graham with his writing and, by doing so, increase his stamina. The following chapter will help you create goals with your students that will drive their learning and maintain their motivation.

Using Conferences to Create Growth-Oriented Goals

Goals are part and parcel of engaged learning and living. Without any destinations, signposts, or aspirations, it can be difficult to find purpose in the work we do every day. We often clean our house a little better when we have an important guest coming (mom) than when it's just another Tuesday. Goals can be measurable and quantifiable, but they do not always have to be so. The goal of vacation could be to see every sight listed in the guidebook, or it could simply be to unwind. Either way, there is purpose and intention to our actions.

The same is true in our classrooms. Instruction needs to be rooted in purpose and intention, and not always our *own*. Part of teaching, as we discuss in Chapter 2, is the ability to see the "you-ness" of each child. Goal setting, as we saw between Ms. Kelly and Graham in Chapter 9, happens in the context of a conversation to ensure the child's intention is recognized and valued. When Kristi met with a personal trainer, the first question the trainer asked was, "What do you want to get out of this process?"

Sometimes when we are asked that question, we are not aware of what the outcomes could be, and a caring professional will suggest options, always giving the final choice to the individual. When Kristi and her husband went to a financial advisor, she sat and explained all the different goals people might have when they invest—a quick increase in money, a slower reliable build toward the future, eventual home ownership or retirement. The financial advisor had informed advice, but she never tried to give the couple the answer. "That," she said, "is up to you."

In the classroom, we suggest using conferences, one-on-one meetings that happen within the structure of workshop teaching (see Chapter 1), to set goals. These conferences are not more than five minutes, and when goal setting is involved, they can follow a particular protocol that values the individual's intentions and choice above all else.

In Your Own Classroom

Setting goals with each individual child will take time, but trust that it is time well spent. Research cited in the previous chapter outlines the efficacy of self-selected goals: adults and children alike are far more motivated when they have some degree of autonomy. We suggest the following steps when setting goals with students:

1. Study the work and talk with the child.
2. Work out the "story" of the goal.
3. Record the goal and keep it close.
4. Build in time for daily celebration and reflection.

SOME NUTS AND BOLTS OF GOAL SETTING

We find we set goals with children early in the fall and then again on an as-needed basis. Aim to cocreate "meaty" goals (see more in the following table "Lean Versus Meaty Goals"), ones that will take four to six weeks to achieve and are descriptive and prescriptive. If this is your first go-around with goal setting, you might start in one area of the day, like writing, and expand as you get more comfortable. If you have been goal setting with children for a while, you might imagine setting goals that cross content areas or more quickly releasing the reins so children set and manage their own goal systems.

Lean Versus Meaty Goals

Subject	Lean Goal (Missing Important Information)	Meaty Goal (Substantial and Engaging for a Longer Duration of Time)
Reading	Visualize what is happening.	When what you're reading gets fuzzy, reread and use all of your senses (sight, hearing, taste, smell, and feeling) to bring what you're reading to life.
Writing	Use feeling words.	Reread and check if you have made a "scene" for your reader. Look for (and add) dialogue, small actions, and setting on every page.
Math	Make sure it makes sense.	When you begin a problem, estimate what the approximate answer will be. Then, check back with that estimate and ask yourself, "Does this make sense?"
Across the day	Use your words to solve problems.	When someone has something you want, use your words to ask for it. Try, "Can I see that when you are done?" If the person says no, take a deep breath and decide if you want to ask again.
	Be more flexible.	When you think you're stuck, think to yourself, "I can be flexible!" and ask yourself, "Is there another way I can do this?"
	Control your negative self-talk.	When you hear those brain gremlins saying things like, "No, you can't!" switch up the talk in your brain and say, "Yes, I can!"

Study the Work and Talk with the Child

Another way to think about bridgeable goals is to consider Vygotsky's zone of proximal development. This zone begins at what the child can do independently and maxes out at the point where the child cannot perform the task, regardless of the level of assistance (Bodrova and Leong 2007, 40). Within this zone are many, many things children can do with assistance, and this is the fertile ground of goals. It takes a study of a child at work as well as ongoing conversations to get a sense of where the child's zone begins and ends, and what the next step for that child should be.

As a teacher, it is incredibly helpful to study the areas where children almost have something: punctuation sporadically placed, dialogue consuming entire pages with no break, and moments of reading fluency broken up by struggle. These "used but confused" moments, as Donald Bear, researcher and author of *Words Their Way*, calls them in word study, are signs that a child has an emerging awareness of something. These flickering skills make powerful reachable goals. We can engage students in conversations around these emerging skills and refine our own understanding of our students' development by asking questions like these:

- What is easy for you?
- What is tricky for you?
- Is there a place where you tried something new? How did you do it?
- Is there something you want to try but are not sure how?
- What is something you are feeling proud of in this work? Why?
- Where were you persistent (flexible, resilient, etc.)?
- It looks like you were trying to ____ ; is that true?

Once the goal is identified for the child, you have only selected a destination. Together, you and the child must map out and record the journey so she has a reasonable, reliable way to achieve her goal again and again.

Work Out the "Story" of the Goal

Carol Dweck, in *Mindset*, argues that the difference in a goal that is met and a goal that isn't is in the completeness of the vision. Dweck suggests that we think of goals as bigger than just a what; she recommends that we also include the how and the when, that we create a "vivid, concrete plan" (2007, 237). We can craft a little story to tell and retell ourselves to better visualize the conditions in which we will be effective in meeting our goal. This is an idea that is pervasive in pop wisdom as well. Walt Disney is quoted as saying, "If you can dream it, you can do it." This idea is also akin to surveying the entirety of a set of Internet-created driving directions before beginning a trip. The clearer the journey, the more likely we are to get to our destination. When creating a clear, bridgeable goal with children, try to include the following (see Figure 10.1 for a diagram of a goal):

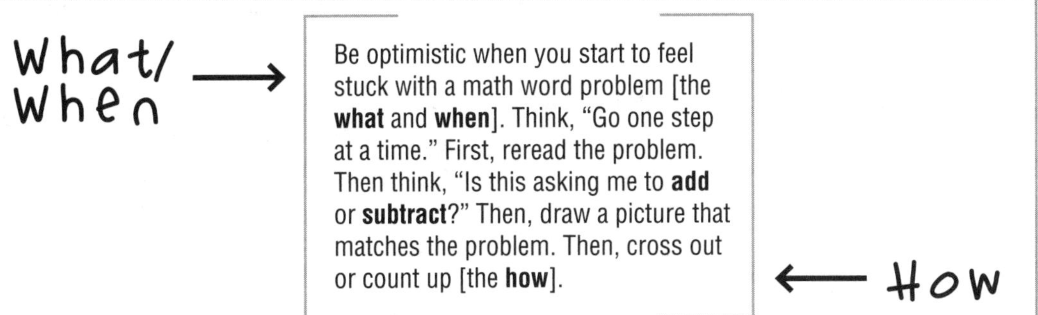

FIGURE 10.1 Diagram of a Goal

- **The What:** Heidi Grant Halverson suggests that when wording a goal, we "think in terms of progress, not perfection" (2013, 80). She says we should "use words like improve, learn, progress, develop, grow, and become" (80). Try to phrase a goal with these action-oriented, effort-embracing words. For example, Graham's goal was to "develop optimism and resilience when [he] hit a wall."
- **The How:** In some circles, the how is referred to as "task analysis," or the breakdown of a complicated task into a few simple steps. The easiest way to discover the best how for a child is to study how the child already approaches the task and to offer suggestions to make it easier or more efficient. It can be easy to step in and say, "Do it this way," but our job is to help the child make sense of a process that will work for him. Think in terms of steps (1, 2, 3, . . .) when crafting this part of the goal. Graham nailed this part of the process, in part because of his previous experience in goal setting. Graham outlined his steps this way:

    1. Think to myself, "I've hit a wall, but I can get over it!"
    2. Get up.
    3. Think about what I need to teach Brandon to make him want to switch to football.
    4. Think about how I can do it.
    5. Do it!

- **The When or the Where:** Visualizing a when (when I finish writing) or where (at the end of every chapter in my book) makes it easier to register that it is time to do the goal. Recipes are masters of this aspect of goal setting: when the cookies brown, when the cheese bubbles, when the dough

> rises . . . these cues signal a behavior, just as when we include a when in our goals. Graham's when? When he hit a wall in writing.

It will take some practice for you and your students to be able to come up with effective goals together (see the box "Working on the 'Co-' in Co-constructed" for answers to predictable problems that come up when co-constructing goals). Once you and your student have created a goal, tell it back like a story (see Chapters 7 and 8 for more about storytelling). Have the child act out the story, practice the goal, or retell the story to you to check on the appropriateness of the goal and the child's understanding. Retelling will not be quite enough to keep the flame of this goal burning, so we recommend engaging the child in a personal record-keeping system also.

Record It and Keep It Close

Fitness wristbands and devices have become ubiquitous in the past few years. Now, it seems, everyone either uses, or knows someone who uses, a fitness tracking device for steps, calories, or active minutes. These devices owe some of their success to their omnipresence. Strapped to our wrists, we can't help but be reminded of our fitness goals. Vygotsky referred to items like these as mediators, items that "prompt a specific response" (Bodrova and Leong 2007, 51). Perhaps the most essential aspect of mediators in the Vygotskian framework is that children must be able to use them independently (63). When having children record goals, it is essential that we ask the children to either write the goals (in their own words) or illustrate the goals (in their own way) so that the cues are personal and meaningful to the children. Graham's visual interpretation of his goal was made easier by the teacher's use of consistent symbols in the classroom.

The mediator should be close to the child when she is working on the task. Sentence-strip bracelets, index-card necklaces, stickies on folders, and portable goal sheets are all ways to keep the child's goal near at hand (see Figure 10.2). For

FIGURE 10.2 A Goal Mediator

the teacher, we recommend keeping goals written on conferring sheets so that you have them close at hand when meeting with students. (See Appendix D for an example conferring sheet.)

WORKING ON THE "CO-" IN CO-CONSTRUCTED

PREDICTABLE PROBLEM 1: THE CHILD'S GOAL IS DIFFERENT FROM THE TEACHER'S GOAL

In goal-setting conferences, it's common for children to come up with a different goal from the teacher's because children may not yet know all the goals they *could* set for their work. In this case, it often helps to get at the *why*. For example, "Why do you want to get better at drawing in your books?" Often the answer to the why provides the teacher a big enough umbrella to offer other avenues of thinking that may be more in line with what the teacher sees as the more pressing need. If a child is highly motivated to reach a particular goal that is not aligned at all with what the teacher believes is pressing, there is great value in having the child work toward it. Setting and meeting a goal is a life skill well worth the time. After the child meets the goal that she is highly invested in, the teacher may then step in to help in planning the next goal so it better aligns with what the child needs (but may not know she needs).

PREDICTABLE PROBLEM 2: THE CHILD HAS NO GOAL IN MIND

If the child is meeting your goal-setting questions with silence or confusion, it can help to rely on a mentor to help the child identify something he might want to get better at. In writing, for example, have a child select a book that he loves and then talk about why. The child may see something the author does that he admires and wants to bring into his writing. A teacher can also offer a menu of possibilities, making sure the final choice ultimately rests with the child.

PREDICTABLE PROBLEM 3: THE CHILD DOES NOT APPEAR TO BE INTRINSICALLY MOTIVATED

Choice is one of the best motivators in the world, so ensuring children choose their goals (with support) often ensures they will be motivated toward meeting them. However, there are cases when children may not appear to be motivated beyond the first day or may quickly lose interest in their self-selected goals. In this case, you may want to build in more time to reflect with the student and celebrate their progress—no matter how small. Before running is self-motivating, completing the run is often what a person celebrates. However, if this still proves ineffective, you and the student may need to revise the goal to be more in line with the child's passions and desires. As teachers, our goal is for students to be engaged, not to trudge along through an unmotivating task just for the sake of completing it.

Build in Time for Daily Reflection and Celebration

Simple routines like tallying each time a student tried his goal (see Figure 10.3), sharing with a partner a place where he was successful, or placing a star sticky note at a place where he would like try the goal the next day increase the visibility of the goal. Some teachers take a few moments to celebrate goals that have been met and keep the evidence to show and celebrate the growth that has occurred over the course of the year. Things that are visible tend to stay in the front of our minds. Setting up a simple three-minute routine that involves reflecting on progress toward a goal (see more on reflection in Chapters 11 and 12) increases the likelihood of meeting and maintaining goals.

FIGURE 10.3 A Goal Card with a Tally Built in

Developing Flexibility in Reading Strategies: Window into First Grade

As reading workshop begins in this first-grade classroom, Kristin heads over to Monica, who has signed up for a conference in one of the open slots for the day (see Figure 10.4).

Kristin settles in next to Monica on the floor and sets her notes to the side for a moment. "How's it going?" she asks.

- It can help to have a conferring schedule posted to keep you on track and keep the students aware of when they will see you.
- Goal-setting conferences can be planned or impromptu.
- For more on the flow of conferring, see the list of resources in Appendix A.

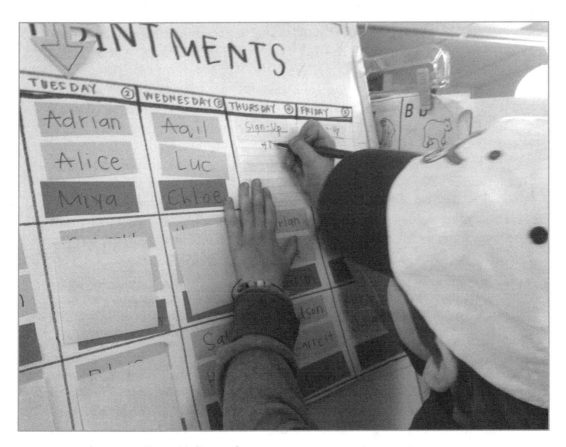

FIGURE 10.4 Conference Sheet with Sign-up Spots

Monica smiles and pulls a book out of her personal baggy. "I wanted to read you my book!" she exclaims excitedly.

Kristin smiles, nods, and asks, "What made you choose this one to read to me?"

"It's really funny and I was really persistent when I was reading it," Monica replies, adding, "and I like it a lot."

- Kristin is letting Monica set the agenda in this conference while still asking questions to get more information about her habits and interests as a reader.
- As your class gains familiarity with the constellation of stances, you will hear the stances pop up more and more in conversations.

"Whoa," Kristin replies, her eyes growing big. "So you know I love funny books, so this was a smart choice, but tell me more about this persistence?!"

Monica smiles and flips a few pages in and shows Kristin a page with a pig in a sled going down a hill. The text reads, "Piggy slides down the hill." "I didn't know this word," Monica says, pointing to *slides*, "so I just tried and tried and tried."

"You tried and you tried?" Kristin asks. "What did that look like? Can you show me?"

Monica starts to read the page, and when she gets to *slides*, she half-mumbles a word with some of the sounds found in *slides* and then ends the sentence with a flourish. Kristin asks to hear it one more time to check her own understanding of Monica's process and Monica, again, mumbles her way through.

Kristin has seen Monica do this before in other texts—as a reader, she heavily relies on sounding out, but for young readers, that is not always the most reliable way to attack a word. In addition, Monica tends to be most excited at the completion of tasks: I am done reading! I finished my writing book! I am the first one done with my story problem! Kristin considers all of this information as she watches Monica.

- Always try to place an event in context: Has this happened before? How does this fit with what I know about this child as a learner and as a person?
- Kristi's doctor once said about a test result, "Once doesn't count; you have to see it twice." The same is true for teaching: look for patterns, not isolated events.

Kristin takes a second to think about what she knows and decides to ask a follow-up question. "Monica, what's the best way to solve a tricky word?'

Monica immediately goes back to the word *slides* and says, "You sound it out!" Kristin has not emphasized this as a strategy for her readers, but she knows that many children hear the phrase from parents and caregivers. Though it is certainly one aspect of tackling words, for beginning readers, who may not yet have a command of all the rules of the language, it is one fraught with challenge. Kristin, unsure of how Monica understands this idea, asks for a demonstration of "sounding it out." In response, Monica delivers the sounds one at a time, resulting in a word that sounds something like "selidess." Monica screws up her face, and Kristin asks her what she is thinking. Monica replies, "That is a weird word!"

- Don't assume; ask for more information or a demonstration if you need to understand what the child is doing.
- All of this has taken about three minutes.

Kristin nods and says, "So, sounding it out is like when we stretch words in writing—we say the sounds and then write the letters?" Monica nods. "Hmm," Kristin continues, "that can be a helpful strategy for solving tricky words, but sometimes, even when we are persistent, it may not always work, huh? We know we have it figured out when it looks right, sounds right, and makes sense, and '*selidess*' didn't quite do that, huh?"

Monica nods and says, "It's not *even a word*!" flinging her hands up.

Kristin smiles and goes on, "You know this makes me think of Iron Man." Monica's eyes light up at the mention of her favorite superhero. "Iron Man is persistent, but even more importantly, he is flexible. Remember how many cool tools he has to help him?"

- Refer back to characters the class knows as models of the stance you are referring to (see Chapter 3 for some examples).

Monica begins to list off everything Iron Man has in his possession, as Kristin nods. Kristen intercepts before the conversation goes completely off topic. "So, you have as many tools as Iron Man when you read, you know. You have lots of ways to figure out a word that makes sense and looks right." Monica gives a slight nod. Kristin continues, "Like using the picture; that is a power, right? Or rereading and thinking about what could fit." Monica is nodding more emphatically as she catches Kristin's drift and adds in a few other tools.

"Sounding out is just *one* tool," Kristin says. "The thing about being a powerful reader is that you have to think like Iron Man—you have to think, 'Huh, what else can I use to figure out this tricky word?' Sometimes we have to change tools. Does that sound like something you might want to work on, being flexible like Iron Man when you read?"

Monica nods and shoots her arms out, miming Iron Man moves. "I am gonna be Iron Man!" she shouts.

- These reading tools have been taught prior to this conference; the goal is not for Monica to do one particular skill better but rather for Monica to be flexible in using her own reading skill set.
- Kristin has done some of the heavy lifting in getting to this goal, but she still asks for confirmation from Monica that this feels like something worth pursuing.

"OK, Iron Monica," Kristin starts, "let's figure out how to do this. First, what should we write it on so you can keep it close?"

Monica points to a cuff another child has on his wrist. "A command cuff!" Monica declares.

Kristin grabs a length of sentence strip and says, "OK, so let's think this through. You are working on being flexible. Can you make the sign for flexible on the cuff?" Monica draws the class sign for flexible (see Chapter 3 for examples) and then waits. Kristin says, "OK, so let's add some power buttons on this cuff. What can you do when you come to a tricky word?"

"Look at the picture!" Monica says.

Kristin asks her to draw something on her cuff that will remind her she can use the picture. "What else?" Kristin asks.

"Reread the page!" Monica declares, starting to draw another icon.

"One more?" Kristin suggests.

"Use the letters!" Monica says as she starts drawing. (See Figure 10.5 for Monica's completed cuff.)

- Kristin uses symbols and icons in all her charts, and many children have internalized them as shortcuts to meaning. This is what Monica is drawing.
- Kristin is letting Monica self-select her strategies so that she can continue to own her goal.

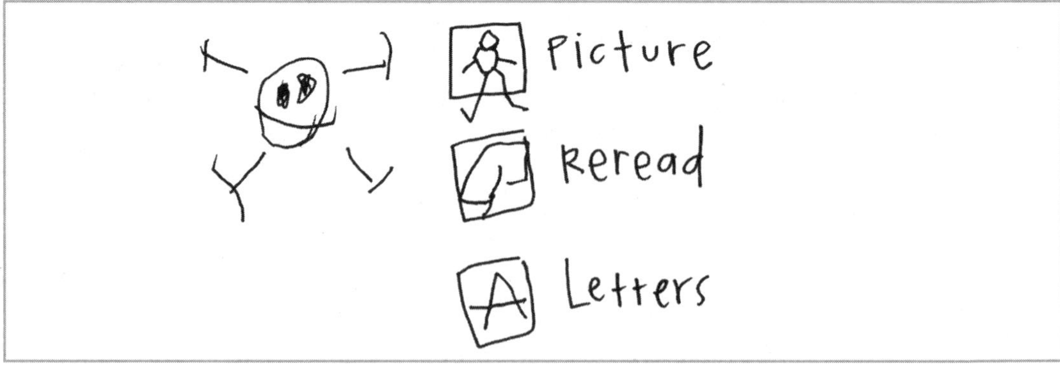

FIGURE 10.5 Monica's "Command Cuff"

"OK," Kristin says, as Monica finishes drawing. "Let's tell this like a story, so we know how to use it." (For more on setting up stories, see Chapters 7 and 8.) "When Iron Monica comes to a tricky word, she activates her flexibility cuff—*beep, boop, beep*—and tries one of her strategies. If it doesn't work, what does Iron Monica do?! Monica hits another button on her cuff and says, 'Use another strategy!'"

Kristin suggests they try it out on Monica's book. When Monica hits *slides*, Kristin whispers, "Try your cuff!" Monica hits her "reread" icon and goes back to the beginning. She gets a good running start before she peters out at "sllll." Monica looks at Kristin and Kristin points to her own wrist. Monica looks down and pushes the button for looking at the picture. Monica looks at the picture and puts her finger on Piggy on the sled and stares for a minute. Kristin whispers, "What's happening?"

Monica looks again and says, "Piggy is sledding. Oh! He is sledding!" She goes back to the page and reads again, "Piggy *sleds* down the hill!"

- Tell the story of the goal using the when (when you come to a tricky word), the what (you can be flexible), and the how (by trying different strategies until it makes sense and sounds right).
- Monica is close but not perfect (she said *sleds* rather than *slides*). Kristin lets this mistake go for now, knowing that readers at Monica's level should really be using beginning and ending sounds along with meaning, which is exactly what Monica has done.

"Woo-hoo," Kristin says. "That made sense, didn't it?" Monica nods, and Kristin asks her to explain how she is going to use the cuff one more time. When Monica is done explaining how she can do it, Kristin offers one last tip. "Every time you use your cuff, you should put a sticky note on that page so you can share with your reading partner all the times you were flexible!" Monica nods and Kristin sits by her side as Monica finishes reading her the book.

Reflecting on and Maintaining Growth

In an interview in *Maximize Your Potential: Grow Your Expertise, Take Bold Risks and Build an Incredible Career*, Joshua Foer explains the three stages of learning development: the cognitive phase (intellectualizing the task, discovering new strategies to perform better, making lots of mistakes); the associative stage (generally doing better, making fewer errors); and, finally, the autonomous stage (turning on autopilot) (2013, 96). The transition between the stages of learning development is subtle and often not recognized by the learner. However, there is a point in our learning where we decide we are good *enough*, and we transition into the autonomous stage, so we can move something new onto the front burner of our mind. This autonomous stage is sometimes referred to as the "OK plateau." Consider things you would claim you are pretty good at: roasting a chicken, driving a car, playing a sport, for example. The difference between us and an expert at these things is that the expert never decided he was good *enough* and never switched on autopilot.

"If you want to get better at something," Foer explains, "you cannot do it in the autonomous stage. One thing that experts in field after field tend to do is use strategies to keep themselves out of that autonomous stage and under their conscious direction" (2013, 97). In other words, to get really good at something, we can never shift into mindless task completion. We have to pick at the skill like a tangled knot, digging and pulling and teasing. As teachers, we must work to communicate this message: it is not what we have sorted out already that is interesting, but the part that remains tangled and troubling that we find worthy of our time and attention. When Kristi wanted to become a runner, not just a casual jogger, she had to look differently at her form, her habits, and her strengths and weaknesses. What was once good enough (naturally breathing) became an area of work (breathing from the stomach, considering when she inhaled and exhaled) to increase her speed and endurance.

We must be careful to couch this message in its context; it is not that someone is never good enough, but rather that there is always something we can refine in an effort to become the best we can be at something. We are never done; we are only ever doing.

Check in Regularly with the Ecosystem of the Classroom

We strive to communicate this message of constant growth in the classroom through the way we talk about goals. When a goal is met, we avoid talking about it like a finish line; instead, we look at it like a mile marker in a much longer journey. When a goal is achieved, we celebrate what we have learned, take a deep breath, survey the scene, and ask, "Now where to?" Sometimes the answer is a refinement of a goal we have just achieved. For example, now that a child uses sticky notes regularly as a reader, she may want to study how she uses stickies and think if there are ways to use them to better assist her as a reader. This classroom message of ongoing development can be supported in a few simple ways:

- **Chart:** Keep charts on class goals, like empathy and flexibility (see Figure 10.6 for an example). Show how large goals can be broken down into smaller steps (the how) to ensure success and growth. Be honest in this work; if progress isn't happening, problem solve with your students to figure out how to make it possible.

- **Role-Play:** Act out situations in and out of the classroom in which kids might encounter challenges and set goals. Goal setting is a life skill, and connecting classroom practice to the greater world enables children to extend this practice. Set up a scenario—"You want to ride a two-wheel bike" or "You want to beat the last level of Angry Birds"—and have children role-play and tell the story of how they will meet that goal. Christine worked with a student who spent day after day planning and role-playing how he would execute a 360 come the winter ski season.

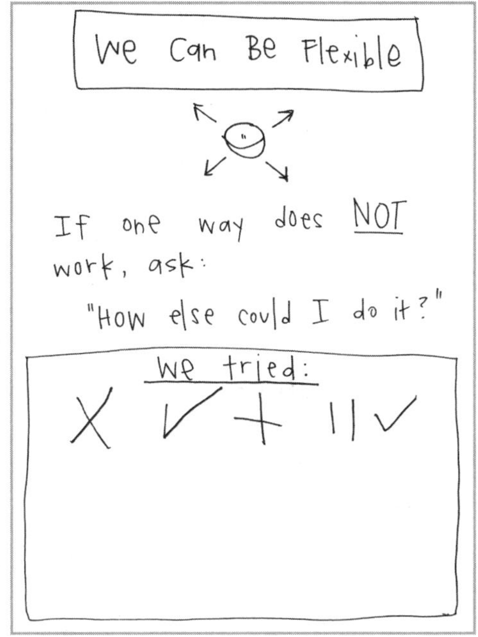

FIGURE 10.6 Flexibility Chart

- **Reflect:** Talk as a class about the growth you've made. Looking at work from early in the year to later on; considering increased stamina, volume, or focus; and even looking at pictures from different parts of the year can help children see the impact of effort on growth.

Check in Regularly with Individual Goal Setting

As soon as possible, we want to hand over the reins of goal setting and maintenance to children. This means our classroom is a place where children set their own goals and we check in and support them as necessary. This transmission of responsibility works well when routines and expectations have been established in the classroom. A teacher's check-in around goals might center on the reasonableness of a goal, the clarity, and the time frame in which the child has been attempting to reach the goal. Through ongoing conferences, we can refine children's goal setting and offer support and encouragement as needed. To establish systems, the following individual scaffolds might be useful:

- **Goal-Setting Frames:** Provide sentence frames that model the necessary parts of a goal: where, when, and how. Children can use these frames until they internalize the structure of a "vivid, concrete plan." For example: *I can _____ when_____ by _______*. The frame should support the whole story of the goal.
- **Stickers:** Give children stickers that they can use to mark where they have attempted, or where they will attempt, their goal. Contrary to stickers as rewards, these stickers serve as visual cues for children to work on their goals. These stickers could be arrows, brains, stars, or anything else that will jog a child's mind to use the goal.
- **Tally Charts:** Children can use charts to record their success in meeting their goals (see Figure 10.7). These can easily be shared with others and used as sources of conversations between teacher and student or partners during independent work time.

Goal setting, and overcoming the "OK plateau," is not a skill developed in isolation. Rather, through feedback and our interaction with others, we become stronger, more engaged, and more energized learners. "Seeking help is a viable cognitive

Goal:

I can use a different strategy when I get stuck on a tricky math problem.

Monday	Tuesday	Wednesday	Thursday	Friday
卌	III	II		

FIGURE 10.7 Student Tally Chart Divided by Days

strategy promoting resilience. It ought not to be confused with dependency, which means relying on a single source excessively over time. But in all learning situations, wherever and whenever obstacles exist, well-motivated learners will access whatever resources are available, and use them to their advantage" (Hattie and Yates 2013, 29). Our role as teachers is to support and help as needed, without veering into dependency, so that children develop the skills needed to navigate the classroom and the world at large. Teaching children how to set goals and make concrete plans to achieve them is teaching children the skills to change the world, one goal at a time.

SUGGESTIONS FOR ENGAGING FAMILIES

- Ask families to make goal setting a part of their day at home, always coming back to the bigger reason of why the child might want to meet a goal. As we mentioned in Chapter 3, a study found "students with a purposeful-learning attitude (who agreed with socially oriented statements like 'I want to become an educated citizen that can contribute to society') scored higher on measures of grit and self-control than classmates who only reported self-oriented motives for learning such as wanting to get a good job or earn more money" (Chen 2014).
- Ask families to let their children hear them talk about and set goals in their own lives. They can engage in conversations about the progress of their own goals and their children's goals.
- Ask caregivers to try to stay away from rewards-based goal setting, even if it seems like the easier option. A child can put a sticker or a tally on a chart to show that he has met a goal (brushing teeth or cleaning up, for example), but those stickers and tallies do not need to add up to trips to the toy store. Instead, counting the tallies together to celebrate growth and effort, or using the newfound free time to read a book together, can be equally as rewarding.

Reflection: The Engine of Growth in Life and Learning

When Kristi and her husband, Geoff, visited the United Kingdom, they rented a car to explore the countryside. Every time Kristi got behind the wheel, after a few minutes of successful driving, the car would invariably begin to drift bit by bit to the left, spawning countless near misses with parked cars, stone walls, bushes, and one very wayward farm animal. With hands clenched on the dashboard, Geoff reached his breaking point after the side mirror came within millimeters of a yet another stone wall. "Kristi," he stammered, "focus!" The thing was, Kristi thought she *was* focusing. She pulled over to the side of the road, which in actuality was just stopping, since she was driving so close to the side anyway, and thought for a minute.

In their book *Learning and Leading with Habits of Mind*, Arthur L. Costa and Bena Kallick describe reflection as the ability to "mentally wander through where we have been and to try to make some sense out of it" (2009, 223). As Kristi replayed her driving in her mind, she realized that her points of focus were all off. When driving at home in New York, she kept her eyes focused slightly to the left of the license plate of the car in front of her. (Next time you are in a car, observe yourself;

you probably do this, too). Now that she was sitting on the right-hand side to drive, keeping the same viewpoint led her off the side of the road. She needed to readjust her focus to the right-hand side of the license plate. Starting the car again, she kept her eyes trained to the right-hand side of the road and the cars ahead of her and, much to the relief of Geoff and farm animals alike, managed the roads with more precision and accuracy.

Much like Kristi's driving, autopilot in learning and life can lead to unintended, and sometimes disastrous, consequences. In psychology, this is called the Einstellung effect: the cost of success is that it can block our ability to see when what has worked well in the past might not any longer (Lewis 2014, 94). Each time Kristi started to drive, she automatically used techniques that had worked for her before, without thinking about why or when they worked. It was only when she stopped and explored her thinking that she saw that the very elements that made her a successful driver at home were almost killing her in the United Kingdom.

All the thinking and work of the previous chapters bring us to this culminating idea: true growth comes from our ability to honestly and purposely reflect on our actions and our learning. When we can hold our thinking in our hands and angle it one way and another, we can see that it is made of parts that can be changed and manipulated to better suit our intentions. Reflection is the engine of growth in all areas of our life. Reflection keeps us from veering into the wrong lane, literally and metaphorically, so that we can better reach the outcomes we seek. Reflection helps us adapt and thrive in a new and changing world.

More Than a Mirror: The Purpose and Power of Reflection

It can be tempting in life to set a pace where we look only forward. Phrases like "rat race" and "race to the top" underscore the idea we should keep our eyes trained ahead and our minds on the future. Yet, research, and life, proves time and time again that moving forward is more successful when we first spend time looking back. In an *Atlantic* magazine article titled "Study: You Really Can 'Work Smarter, Not Harder,'" Nanette Fondas (2014) lays out research that found time spent reflecting (synthesizing, articulating the key points) on what was learned immediately after the learning improved both retention and future performance.

The article covers two different studies, led by researchers from HEC Paris, Harvard Business School, and the University of North Carolina, which found that deliberate time spent reflecting after a problem or lesson aided in the subjects' performance the next time they confronted a similar task. Fondas writes: "In the field study, groups of newly-hired customer-service agents undergoing job training were compared. Some were given 15 minutes at the end of each training day to reflect on the main things they had learned and write about at least two lessons. Those given time to think and reflect scored 23 percent better on their end-of-training assessment than those who were not. And these improvements weren't temporary—they lasted over time, researchers found." Reflection allows us to flag our new learning, highlighting a more efficient and effective pathway to follow in the future.

If, as teachers, our goal is that students really and truly learn, we must make routine reflection an essential aspect of our classrooms. If using a constellation of stances for energized and engaged learning and living is a goal for our students, then we must give them time to reflect on those as well. We must build classrooms where before we move to the next thing, we spend time marinating in the "now" thing. In their chapter "Learning Through Reflection" in *Learning and Leading with Habits of Mind*, Arthur L. Costa and Bena Kallick describe reflective classrooms as ones where teachers ensure "students are fully engaged in the process of making meaning. They organize instruction so that students are the producers, not just the consumers, of knowledge" (2009, 222). Reflection is a critical aspect of constructing understanding; exploring why and when and how things work or don't work ensures children are active and agential problem solvers. Teaching is always more than imparting information; it is a way to transmit a way of being in the world: curious, reflective, and active.

In fact, reflective classrooms ask students to "reflect on their learnings, to compare intended with actual outcomes, to evaluate their metacognitive strategies, to analyze and draw causal relationships, and to synthesize meanings and apply their learnings to new and novel situations. Students know they will not 'fail' or make a 'mistake,' as those terms are generally defined. Instead, reflective students know they can produce personal insight and learn from *all* their experiences" (Costa and Kallick 2009, 223). It is this aspect of reflection, the ability to reframe and redefine failure, that draws us, as teachers interested in developing students' whole beings, in for closer and more thoughtful study.

Failure Redefined: Risk Is the Birthplace of Innovation

I have not failed, I've just found 10,000 ways that won't work.

—THOMAS EDISON, as quoted in *The Rise*, by Sarah Lewis

Think about a time you failed, really failed. It's hard to come up with one, isn't it? We can think of things we have struggled through, things that taught us lessons, but have we really and truly failed? Sarah Lewis, in her book *The Rise*, explains it thusly: "The word failure is imperfect. Once we begin to transform it, it ceases to be that any longer. The term is always slipping off the edges of our vision, not simply because it's hard to see without wincing, but because once we are ready to talk about it, we often call the event something else—a learning experience, a trial, a reinvention—no longer the static concept of failure" (2014, 10–11). Failure is not ever nearly as devastating as we fear; we move through it, often the better for it.

In fact, psychologists Gilbert and Wilson have found that people have a "psychological immune system" of sorts that protects our sense of self and helps us fight against perceived mental threats, according to Michael Schwalbe (2013, 189–90). It is a process in our own mind that helps us find meaning in setbacks, rationalize our actions, and recover from mistakes. According to these psychologists, "we underestimate our resilience" (Schwalbe 2013, 189–90). Failure, as it is often defined, does not hurt us nearly as much as fear of failure might. While we learn from reflecting on our failures, the *fear* of failure means we never try in the first place, and without that, how can the children we teach outgrow themselves?

As teachers, we want to help children fail *successfully*. But what does that mean? It means setting up just-right challenges that will provide opportunities for reasonable struggles so that children will encounter difficulty. If the difficulty level of our provided opportunity is too great, the child will not learn that she has the personal resources to overcome challenge. If the difficulty level is too easy, the child will not have a chance to reflect and grow from the process. (See Chapter 1 for more on setting up just-right challenges.) Reflecting on the challenges we face, and the lessons we learn from that, gives us the strength to face future struggle with confidence. Reasonable risk is as essential to growth as water and air.

What is at stake when we withhold risk from children? According to some researchers that study children's play, long-term issues can arise from preventing children from taking reasonable, just-right risks. "By engaging in risky play, children are effectively subjecting themselves to a form of exposure therapy, in which they force themselves to do the thing they're afraid of in order to overcome their fear. But if they never go through that process, the fear can turn into a phobia. Paradoxically, Sandseter writes, 'our fear of children being harmed,' mostly in minor ways, 'may result in more fearful children and increased levels of psychopathology.'" (Rosin 2014). Allowing children space to explore safely, in both free play and learning, helps children learn that risk is the birthplace of potential. This is true for adults too. The Mayo Clinic created an award called the Queasy Eagle after "their Innovation Work Group realized that a lower tolerance for failure might preclude medical breakthroughs" (Lewis 2014, 30). In the year after this initiative to honor "near wins" there were 245 new ideas. With the reframing of failure comes a fertile ground for growth.

Risk, failure, and reflection are three legs of a tripod; without any one of the elements, the tripod falls. Failure is inherent in risk, but through reflection, failure ceases to be an endpoint; instead it is a way station, a chance to take stock, examine the map, make a new plan, and move forward with more knowledge. An old chess adage holds, "A bad plan is better than no plan." It is only through the dual experience of action and reflection that we find the best plans in learning and living.

When Persistence Alone Isn't Enough: Window into Second Grade

Jeff's class has gathered in a circle on the rug, as it often does, for a conversation. These conversations often happen in the morning, but today Jeff sees a reason to reconvene on the rug during a science experiment with force and motion. The inquiry period is midway through, and Jeff has been conferring and working with students for the ten minutes they've had to build a catapult. Out of the corner of his eye, he has watched a few groups of students struggle to build their catapults. Jeff thinks this struggle might make for an interesting conversation, and he has stopped the work so the class could come to the rug to talk.

Jeff hovers in his place outside the circle and begins, "Friends, I stopped you for a minute so that we could have a conversation about something I am noticing happening as we build our structures."

- You may have a set time to hold conversations, or they might happen organically throughout the day.
- Circles work well for conversations so the students can see each other.
- Staying outside of the circle, as a teacher, sends a powerful message that children are talking to *each other*, not the teacher.

"But before we start this conversation, I just want to remind you of one of the things we have been working on as speakers and thinkers," Jeff continues. "When someone is talking, we try to clear our mind of what we were planning to say, so we have space to hear what the speaker is telling us. Then, we think, 'What can I say back to *that*?'" Jeff gestures as he speaks, pretending to push ideas out of his head and nodding thoughtfully as though listening. "Otherwise," he says, "we end up with conversations like that one I had with Ryan, where I said, 'What do you want for dinner?' and he said, 'Yesterday.'" The class laughs at this familiar story Jeff has told about he and his husband and the perils of not listening. Jeff then taps the little drawing taped to the easel of someone clearing his mind that a student has drawn to illustrate this concept (see Figure 11.1).

- You can start conversations by framing a goal for the speaking and listening. These goals take multiple conversations to master, and Jeff is revisiting a recent one.
- Talking about real-life conversations helps children see the real-life purpose of these skills.
- One way to build a warm relationship with students is to share stories of your own life.

FIGURE 11.1 Student Drawing of "Clearing Your Mind to Listen"

"OK, we have some friends who ran into trouble, and so we are going to help them reflect a little and see if we can help," Jeff says, nodding to Samira and Alex, whom he has already prepped to start the conversation. "Ready to start us talking?"

Samira and Alex look at each other and have a brief debate of "you go first" before Samira takes the lead. "Every time we tried to build our catapult, it would just fall apart." A chorus of "me, toos" echo around the circle, and Jeff crouches behind some of the students, nodding and jotting a few notes down.

- Teachers can start the topic or prepare students to start the topic, as Jeff has.
- Blend as much into the background as possible and jot notes. (See Appendix B for a note-taking form for conversations.)

The circle is quiet for a while and Jeff sits and waits for a minute to see who might step into the silence. His patience is rewarded when Duru pipes up, "But how did it fall apart?"

Samira begins trying to explain, using phrases like "this part" and "that thing" and everyone appears a bit confused.

Charlie throws his hands up in exasperation and says, "I have *no* idea what you are talking about!"

Samira quickly gets the pieces, and she and Alex attempt to assemble the catapult. As the top bar falls off again, Alex exclaims, "Like that! That's what happens all the time." (See Figure 11.2.)

The children all watch as Samira and Alex attempt to put the catapult together again. Jeff leans in to whisper into the ear of the child in front of him, "Ask them what they did when it fell."

FIGURE 11.2 The Collapsing Catapult

The child asks, and Samira answers, waving her arms, "We tried it again and again and again!" demonstrating balancing the bar and having it collapse.

"That's persistence!" Max says from his perch on the other side of the rug. Other kids nod in assent.

Alex drily replies, "Persistence isn't making it work!"

- Jeff's class has already worked hard on ensuring that only one voice talks at a time. If your class struggles with this, you might try some of the techniques described in the section "Addressing Common Issues to Make Conversations More Effective" in Chapter 12.
- "Whispering in," or prompting a child to ask a question, can help move the conversation along without moving the focus to the teacher.

Jeff jumps on this line to pause the conversation, knowing part of his job in this conversation is to help kids focus on big ideas. For the first time since this conversation began a few minutes ago, Jeff stands up, drawing all eyes to him. "Whoa," he begins, "that is a big idea. Let me see if I can say it another way. Samira and Alex, can you let me know if I say this right? OK, so persistence—trying the same thing again and again—doesn't always mean you figure something out?"

Alex cuts in, "Yeah, we kept trying it the same way, but it still kept falling." Samira nods in agreement.

Jeff looks at the rest of the circle and asks, "Friends, is it true that sometimes when you try something again and again, it doesn't always work out? Can you think of a time when that has been true or not true? Turn and talk to someone near you."

- Use your intervention purposefully and sparingly to draw attention to big ideas and to help steer the conversation. Rudders adjust direction from the back of a boat; likewise, your teaching should help shift conversations subtly and only as needed.
- Using turn-and-talks periodically in conversations makes sure everyone's voice is heard by someone.
- Note that Jeff is leaving behind the science-experiment aspects of this conversation to instead focus on the stances of energized and engaged learning.

As Jeff listens to conversations, he taps one or two students and asks if they would be willing to share what they said with the whole group. As he brings the class' attention back to the circle, he nods at Devonte, cueing him to share his story.

"So one time when I was trying to beat Angry Bird, I kept shooting the bird to the same spot on the tower because I thought that would knock it down. I did it, like, one million times, and I *never* knocked it down. And then my brother showed me that you had to knock this *other* part of the tower down, and I was like, 'Ohhhhhhhhh,' and then I did that and beat the level." A chorus of voices go up at this story, some asking about which level and which Angry Birds iteration, others agreeing, others trying to jump in with their own stories. Devonte regains control by saying, "Wait, wait, one voice! I don't know what you are saying!" The class sits back and a bunch of thumbs pop up along the rim of the circle, the symbol for wanting to share when many people want to share. Devonte points to Sasheer.

Sasheer uses this opportunity to jump in and share a similar experience with trying to ollie her skateboard and then getting it only when she moved her feet a little differently.

Lucas adds in his own experience of wanting to jump from a playground platform and reach the monkey bars, but he kept missing because he couldn't jump far enough, no matter how long he tried.

"Wait, so what is the big idea here?" Jeff asks. "What is the same about all of these stories?"

The class is silent for a second until Monica pipes up, "If you do something the same all the time, sometimes it won't work. You have to be flexible or sometimes just not do it."

Murmurs of agreement go around the circle and Jeff directs them back to the catapult. "So," he says, "what should we do about the problem some of us are having with the catapults?"

- Teach children strategies they can use when the conversation seems to veer out of control.
- Jeff is steering the conversation toward future action and away from pure retelling. In this way he is providing a model of reflection—you learn from what didn't work (or what did).

"Well," Alex says, "we should probably try to build it a different way, since the same way isn't working."

"You could use a rubber band to hold the spoon on," offers Lucas, "since that is the part that keeps falling off."

"Or maybe tape, too; you could see which one works better," Kalen adds.

Alex and Samira nod and Jeff gives everyone a chance to turn and talk to make a plan for what the students will do next with their catapults. Then, he brings everyone back to looking at him. Jeff says, "We had an idea here today that is even more important than catapults, something that will help us in the world. When we are being persistent and it's just not working, sometimes we need to be flexible and try something different. We can ask for advice, or study what is happening and try to fix it, but just doing the same thing again and again often leads us to frustration. We have to find what is not working and learn from it. Can you try to say that same idea to someone next to you in your own words?" Jeff listens in and has a few children say their own interpretations out loud.

Before sending the children back to their catapult designs, Jeff asks for one last reflection. "Friends, how did you do on your open-mind listening today? Give me a thumbs-up if you were able to try to talk back to the idea someone said, instead of just saying your own idea first." Jeff surveys the thumbs-ups and nods. "I agree! Lots of listening and replying to what the person said! Back to your catapults, friends!"

Before letting Samira and Alex get back to work, Jeff grabs them and asks if they could make a reminder sign for the classroom (see Figure 11.3).

- Aim to summarize the current status of the conversation, or have the students summarize the big ideas at the end to help secure the information in their minds.
- Also check in on the goal of the conversation, not the content, and reflect on the success of a particular goal.

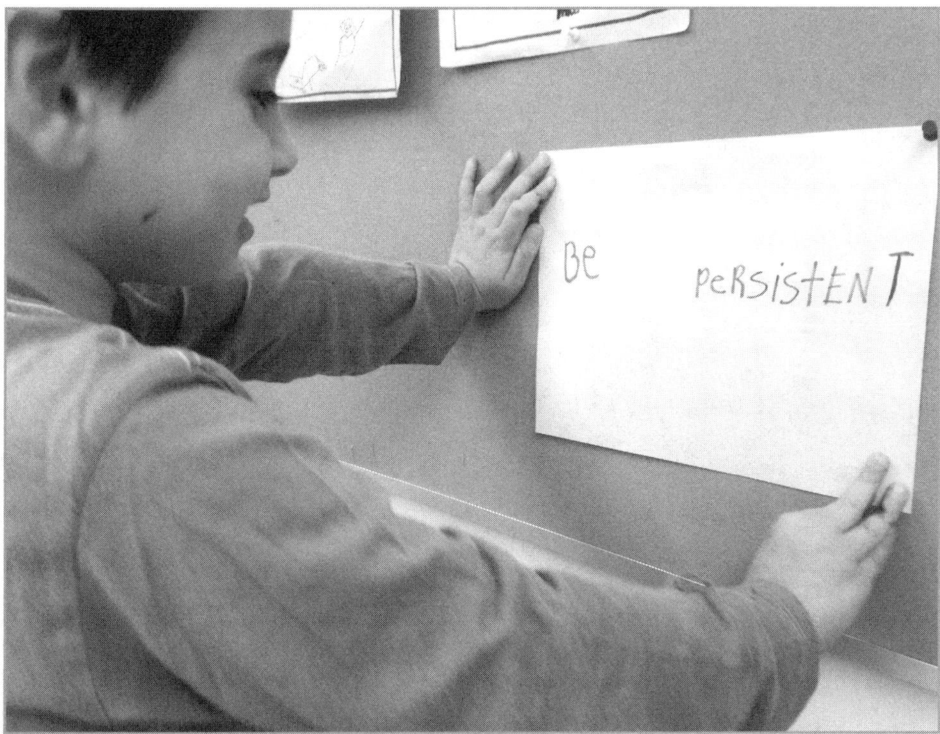

FIGURE 11.3 Reminder Sign for Using Persistence

Moving from Idea to Action

Reflection, like many things, is a habit, a choice of how to live life. There are numerous sayings on the value of reflection: Those who do not study history are doomed to repeat it; an unexamined life is not a life worth living; look back to look forward. These sayings admonish us from keeping our eyes trained only forward. It is the study of how we got to where we are that helps us move strategically and purposefully forward. Time made for reflection is time made for learning; time made for reflection is time made for understanding that failure is part of growing.

The reflective classroom values the journey as much as it values the destination because it is on the journey that we learn who we are in the world. The next chapter will take you through the steps of building a reflective community of energized and engaged learners.

Using Whole-Class Conversations to Build Habits of Constructive Reflection

In *Daring Greatly*, Brené Brown (2012) writes about the "gremlins" that fill our heads when we're feeling especially vulnerable. It's easy, after we've made a mistake, to have the focus of our reflection be on what went wrong, on how we failed. It's too easy for those little gremlins to say, "You know you'll fail again!" The key, according to Brown, is to reach out. By connecting with others who have had similar experiences, by hearing their stories, we will be better able to mute the gremlins and get to the positive, powerful work of reflection.

In our classrooms, creating a space for collective, community reflection helps maintain a balance between thinking through what went wrong and thinking about how things will go better the next time. Whole-class conversations can simultaneously build community (and help dispel feelings of isolation and vulnerability) and build ideas. In *Learning and Leading with Habits of Mind*, Arthur Costa and Bena Kallick note, "External sharing of reflections is important because this kind of reflection multiplies the learning for each individual. As students review the learning events that have taken place, they give their learning new meaning. The opportunity to share often validates a student's internal conversation" (2009, 234). Once a student hears an echo of "me, toos," as Alex and Samira did in Jeff's classroom, the gremlins have a tendency to shrink back into their hiding places.

These community reflections are structured very much like the "grand conversations" that many teachers use to discuss literature, or whole-class talks about social studies, science, or math. In our classrooms, in a given week, we may have grand conversations about a read-aloud, a social problem that needs solving, a science inquiry, and a new math concept. Some of these weave in the constellation of stances and some are purely content driven. Our suggestions for whole-class conversations are grounded in what we know works well in all of these contexts.

Essential Components of Conversations

- Conversations begin with a highly engaging and relevant question or provocation.
- The emphasis should be on student-led discourse; the teacher should take a backseat.
- Students and teachers follow established norms and actively work to build both conversational skills and content-based ideas. (See the Common Core State Standards for speaking and listening for suggestions on skills for your grade.)

Building our students' agency, you might have noticed, has been a thread throughout this book. By using whole-class conversations for reflection, we create yet another opportunity for our children to be agents of their own learning and understanding. In a whole-class conversation, the teacher is not the all-knowing being at the center of attention, but rather a figure on the periphery, as we saw with Jeff, guiding his students to their own aha moment. As Peter Johnston describes in *Choice Words* (2004), this process of "revealing" a strategy or idea is contrasted with "telling" your students an idea. Allowing students to reveal an idea for themselves through conversation deepens their learning and strengthens a sense of community. Additionally, according to Johnston, "naturalizing this sort of conversation opens the possibility that students will continue such conversations among themselves" (2004, 32). Jeff wanted his students to explore a scenario where persisting just wasn't working. He could have simply sat them down and told them, "When you try and try and it still doesn't work, study what is going wrong and be more flexible." But by allowing his students to reflect on the problem, build a collective understanding, and develop an idea themselves, Jeff increased both his students' agency and the likelihood that they would use this concept in the future.

In Your Own Classroom

Although whole-class reflections are student led and somewhat open-ended, the most powerful and effective conversations follow a certain flow. We suggest the follow steps for orchestrating whole-class reflection:

1. The conversation launches with a question or scenario.
2. The talk transitions from what happened to a big idea.
3. The students create a plan for the future.

Balance the Content and the Components of the Conversation

As you saw in Jeff's whole-class conversation, he and his students were balancing and monitoring two parallel threads throughout each part of the conversation: the content of what was being said and how it was being said—that is, the conversation itself. In any whole-class conversation, the content and the quality of the conversation go hand in hand. Every time you have a conversation, pick one element of good conversations to focus on (see the following table "Addressing Common Issues to Make Conversations More Effective" for ideas).

- **Before the conversation begins**, set your intention with the students. Connect to the work the students have been doing in previous conversations. You may want to write the intention down or draw a sketch in a place where the children can see it. Jeff reminded his students to listen so they could respond to what a speaker was saying.
- **As the conversation unfolds**, coach students to practice this skill by whispering to one child, referring back to your visual aid, or pausing the conversation altogether to remind the class of the skill you are focusing on.
- **To wrap up the conversation**, you might ask children to quickly think back on how they did. You could, as Jeff did, ask them to give a thumbs-up if they were able to try out the conversational move.

Addressing Common Issues to Make Conversations More Effective

Issue	Temporary Scaffolds
Everyone talks at once.	• Use a talking stick or ball to slow down the voices and have one person talk at a time. • Teach children a signal to use when they are done sharing their idea.
The conversation stalls out quickly.	• Teach children to ask questions ("Tell us more about that" or "Why?"), to ask for clarification ("I think you're saying ______; is that right?"), or to disagree respectfully ("I hear what you're saying, but . . ."). • Take a moment to turn and talk, or stop and jot, or stop and act to get students to rehearse their ideas one-on-one or alone before speaking in front of the whole group.
Some children participate much more than others.	• Teach children to monitor how much they're talking with a quick tally on a sticky note. Remind them that conversations are about contributions, not domination. • Explicitly teach phrases that invite quiet children to speak, such as, "What do you think?"
Some children are more reluctant to speak.	• Make a personal tool with questions or prompts to use in conversation (see Figure 12.1). **FIGURE 12.1** A Personal Conversation Tool • Give concrete materials to a hesitant child (like a page from a book or the student's own notes) to help the child feel confident enough to share.

Launch a Conversation with a Question or Scenario

The prompts or scenarios that launch your whole-class conversations will vary depending on your class, your grade level, and even the time of year. In September you might have a whole-class conversation about how a specific stance that you've just introduced could be generalized and transferred across academic areas. Readers who developed flexibility in word solving may discover, through conversation, the value of flexibility when problem solving in math. In March, you might meet to reflect on what self-talk moves are especially good at building independence. In May you might meet to reflect on how goals can be transferred to lives outside of school; the optimism a child developed in the classroom around writing could be discussed in relation to an upcoming summer camp that a child will be attending for the first time. The hard-won gains of energized and engaged learning should be extended to energized and engaged living outside the classroom.

No matter the time of the year, you will likely see many moments (or series of moments) bubble up that are worth thinking about more deeply and reflecting on as a whole class. In the second-grade example in Chapter 11, Jeff noticed something interesting happening in a partnership and used it as a springboard into a conversation about the limitations of persistence. In the fifth-grade story that appears later in this chapter, Megan notices a concerning pattern of behavior in her students, and rather than lecture them, she opens the door to a reflective and thought-provoking conversation.

When launching a class conversation designed for thoughtful reflection on behalf of the students, you could frame the topic of the conversation as a question ("What do you think of . . . ?" or "I wonder why . . ."), or you could present a scenario for students to think about ("I noticed that . . ." or "I just saw something really interesting/tricky/exciting. . . ."). Eventually, you'll want your students to take the lead in launching the reflection, as Jeff did, coaching them gently into telling their stories.

As students start to rethink the scenario or discuss the question, you might whisper in a question or offer a suggestion, but the work of retelling is primarily in the hands of the students involved. In Jeff's classroom, Samira and Alex described (and then demonstrated) how they struggled over and over again, trying to get a specific part of their catapult to work. These retellings do not need to be long or dramatic stories; they are just meant to set the stage for what's to come.

Transition from What Happened to a Big Idea

There is something very magical about aha moments. These moments come when we're rereading a failed recipe ("Oh yes, one *cup* of sugar, not a tablespoon."),

TIPS FOR GETTING THE CONVERSATION STARTED

- Have your students sit in a circle, either on the rug or in chairs. It's vital that every student can see every other student, even if this means pushing back tables and chairs for the time being.
- You can choose a specific time of day for these reflective gatherings (perhaps after lunch or at the close of the day) or you can call your class together in the moment, as Jeff did.
- Set aside at least fifteen to twenty minutes or so for these conversations. If a conversation wraps up early, you can always fill the time, but you don't want to cut your students off just as they get to a big idea.
- Present the question or scenario and then step back and allow for wait time. (Really! Count to ten in your head, slowly.)
- As the teacher, sit a bit away from the circle so that you can move around the circle to give little coaching pointers to students and so that you are less of the center of attention. Students should be looking at their classmates as they have this conversation.

when we're trying to figure out how best to reteach a concept that didn't quite work ("Maybe we can have them act it out!"), or when we're trying not to drive into picturesque stone walls in the English countryside ("Look to the right of the license plate, not the left!"). For reflection to be a true complement to risk and failure, there must be some element of learning as an outcome. There must be some aha moment that can lead us down a different path when we take that risk again.

The heart of a reflective whole-class conversation comes when students make this turn from rehashing to reflecting on what can be learned. As students talk through what went wrong (or right) or what stances they were using or what they were thinking, they will eventually (with practice, modeling, and prompting) land on a big idea or an aha moment. Often these big ideas are rather subtle. It is the role of the teacher to have the class pause and think about them. In Jeff's class a big idea (for children and adults alike) was born out of the almost offhand utterance "Persistence isn't making it work!" Jeff achieved a balance between allowing the children to discover a new idea and giving them additional opportunities to think it over, test its validity, and make it their own. The box "Teacher Prompts to Nudge Students Toward Big Ideas" lists several ways that you can support students as they build on an aha moment to create new learning.

TEACHER PROMPTS TO NUDGE STUDENTS TOWARD BIG IDEAS

- Turn and talk about another time this is true.
- Think of books or characters that this idea fits with.
- Rephrase this idea in your own words.
- How does this connect to other stances or habits of mind?
- What does this idea teach us about the world?
- What does this idea make us think about what people should or should not do?

Remember that aha moments do not need to be completely revolutionary, never-before-thought-of ideas; they just need to be ideas that lead your students or your classroom community to see things a little differently. We all come to understandings in our own time (how many times have you said, "Oh, *now* I get it"?), and reflective conversations allow multiple times and multiple entry points for children to construct meaningful understandings.

Create a Plan for the Future

In the final phase of the reflection, the conversation shifts to "Now what?" and students begin to make a plan for the future. In Jeff's class, his students were trying to remember that persistence alone is not a surefire solution to a problem. Jeff summed up the discussion for the class: When you're persistent, but something's not working, study what it is and see if you can be flexible and make it work.

Wrap up your conversation by having your students prepare themselves to risk and fail again. You're collectively saying, "All right, let's give this a try and meet right back here to see if it works." In this way, your students can turn into researchers and your classroom can become their very own lab.

Ways to Extend the Learning

- Read books to find examples of this new idea.
- Have children stop and notice future scenarios where the idea applies and see if the idea holds true.
- Take photographs and tell stories about times when the idea was reinforced. (See Chapters 7 and 8 for more on storytelling.)
- Create a quick visual or chart to remind students of the idea.

Taking Empathy from Theory into Practice: Window into Fifth Grade

It's mid-March, just after lunch, and Megan's class noisily walks into the classroom and settles at the meeting area. Megan trails behind the class, talking quietly with Zadie and Jahirah, whose eyes are red and puffy. Earlier in the week Megan had had a conversation with a different pair of fifth graders about rumors and gossip that were being spread that portrayed other students in a negative light. Megan knows that children at this age try out different identities, and belonging to a group, sometimes at the expense or exclusion of others, becomes a thing of utmost importance. As Megan checks in with the girls at the end of the line, it becomes clear that these behaviors have become a pattern, and it's time to address it as a class.

Megan sits down in her rocking chair and looks out at her class. "Fifth graders," she says calmly. "I noticed today that some members of our class are returning from lunch really, really unhappy. And today isn't the first day that this has happened." She pauses and looks around at the class. Some students nod, a few steal glances at Zadie and Jahirah, but most just look into their laps or at someone nearby.

"Today we're going to pause on reading aloud *Number the Stars.* Instead we're going to circle up and have a real, honest conversation about what has been happening."

The class looks up at Megan and a few groan audibly. She waits for a moment and says quietly, "I know this is hard. It feels pretty uncomfortable to have real, honest conversations. But I can tell you from my own experience, that sometimes the most challenging conversations are the most important ones."

- As teachers, we know that curriculum demands and time constraints can make it feel tempting to ignore the social issues that are festering just below the surface of your classroom ecosystem. But when issues of kindness, respect, and empathy come to a certain point, we have found that the entire ecosystem of the class is so disturbed that no real learning will be accomplished without addressing the issues first.
- When you're entering into whole-class conversations about empathy, don't gloss over the fact that these conversations are not easy, even for adults. Megan has been working all year to create a classroom culture where her fifth graders feel safe enough to have these hard conversations.

Megan leans in close and looks around at her class, trying to make eye contact with every student. "I'll tell you something else: sometimes when we're in an intense conversation, we can say the first thing that comes to our mind and then—*bam*—it's out there in the world and we're left with this pit in our stomach. That's our emotional brain reacting. Today, let's set the intention of taking a breath and letting our emotional brain be influenced by our logical brain before we say something. Can we practice that?"

Megan looks around at her students and they nod.

Wanting to be a little more specific, Megan lays out steps that they will take as they work toward this speaking and listening objective. She says, "We'll take a breath, pause, and think, 'What do I really want to say?' and *then* say it." Megan writes these steps quickly on the whiteboard:

1. Breath and pause.
2. Think carefully.
3. Speak carefully.

- When you're naming a conversational skill that the students will be working on, frame it in a real context so students know that it's generalizable to conversations that they'll have outside of school and throughout their lives.
- Give specific steps that can help students access the skill they are practicing, and record the steps somewhere visible so they can refer to them throughout the conversation.

Megan pauses. "OK. Let's circle up. Zadie, can you start us off by telling your class what you told me in the hall?"

The class quickly forms a circle and Megan grabs a clipboard and sits just outside the circle.

Zadie takes a deep breath and begins, "Everyone just keeps saying that I hate someone else now because I didn't invite her to my sleepover. But I don't. I just knew she was going to be at her dad's and wouldn't be able to come. But now that person won't talk to me. It just feels so unfair when you keep hearing the same thing over and over and it's just not true."

The class is silent for several moments and Megan just quietly writes a note on her clipboard.

Jahirah pipes up: "Yeah, and at recess everyone was telling everyone else that I like this boy from the other fifth-grade class and I don't even know him."

Eduardo raises his shoulders, holds up his hands, and adds, "Yeah but last week you guys were telling everybody that I was going to cry after we lost the basketball game." He looks around at the class. No one makes eye contact.

"It's like everyone is telling rumors about everyone else and we're all mad about it, but no one will stop," Michael says, raising his voice a little.

Megan notes the new word *rumors* and looks over at Michael. "Michael," she says, "can you explain that word, *rumor*, just so we're all on the same page?"

Megan lets the class take charge of the conversation, but when Michael uses a specific word to describe the problem the class is discussing, she takes the opportunity to focus the class on that word. By understanding the word *rumor*, the children can better understand and relate to Michael's experience.

"Rumors are things people spread around. Things that aren't true. Lies."

"Lies that make you feel terrible," Zadie says, crossing her arms.

Megan feels the rising tension and decides to shift the conversation. She leans in to the circle and says quietly, "Fifth graders, remember that words can make you feel things—I know I'm feeling lots of things—but let's pause for a moment and take three deep breaths before we continue our conversation." Megan lowers her head and takes three breaths. She continues, "We've been talking a lot about empathy this year—about thinking about how someone else feels and letting that change your thoughts and actions. Take a second to think about how empathy might relate to what we're talking about right now. I'm going to pass out sticky notes and pencils; be ready to jot down some ideas."

FIGURE 12.2 A Student Reflecting in a Notebook

Megan circulates as students take some quiet, independent reflection time and write notes (see Figure 12.2). She marks a couple of names on her clipboard.

Balancing time for personal reflection during a whole-class conversation can calm heightened emotions and allow quieter children a chance to express their thoughts.

When most student seem to be finished writing, Megan says, "Sasha, can you share what you've jotted, please?"

Sasha reads: "Rumors don't feel bad unless they're about you. They happen so fast you don't think about how another person would feel if they found out."

Megan nods. "How about you, JJ?"

JJ leans over his note and reads, "If you were really thinking about the person, you wouldn't tell lies about them."

Megan says, "I think we've come to a really big, tricky idea here. Rumors swirl and spread so fast that you don't take time to think about how the person you're talking about would feel—about how *you* feel when a rumor is spread about you. And you feel really, really bad, don't you?"

Several members of the class nod in agreement.

"So let's shift and think now about next steps," Megan continues. "Let's put this idea of empathy into action. I'm going to sit back again and I'd like you all to come up with a step-by-step process for what to do when you are told a rumor about someone else." Megan picks up a whiteboard marker and sits away from the circle, ready to write on the easel.

- Name the big idea explicitly and then shift the work of the conversation to what should come next. For older students, the metacognitive work required to think about their thinking can lead to some of the most fruitful and transferable results of the reflection.

The class sits silently for almost a minute. Megan writes a number one on the whiteboard.

"Don't talk about people behind their backs?" Sasha wonders.

"Yeah, but you can say nice things when they're not there," Jahirah counters. "So maybe, don't say bad things about other people?"

"Yeah and when they're not true it's *really* bad," Michael says.

Megan writes, "1. Think: Is this a rumor?"

- The class is still taking charge of the conversation, but Megan is crafting the "How to Deal with Rumors" steps to make them clear and usable.

"Yeah," says JJ, glancing down at his sticky note. "And think about how you would feel if the rumor was about you."

Megan writes, "2. Think: How would I feel?"

"And then don't keep telling people," Charlie says.

Megan writes, "3. Don't tell other people."

"Maybe," Megan adds, "if you're feeling really brave, you can tell the person to stop spreading rumors." She draws a quick stop sign under the number three.

Megan caps the marker and sits back down in her rocking chair. "Well, that wasn't a very easy conversation, was it?" Megan asks honestly. "But it was a start. This is empathy in action. And let me tell you, it's hard stuff. Lots of adults are *still* working on it and we'll keep working on this all year." Megan picks up the read-aloud novel and says, "Let's keep investigating more ways to solve this problem. I wonder if we can find examples in the books we read, in movies we watch, or in songs. Let's keep a running list on this chart."

"Zadie," Megan asks, "will you copy our how-to list onto this chart? We can add the books and movies and songs below."

This conversation by no means fixed every problem and stopped every rumor. But as the fifth graders transitioned to their seats for word study, there was sense that just by laying the issue on the table, and making a tentative plan for moving forward, the students had lifted some of the weight from their shoulders.

Reflecting on and Maintaining Growth

> *The chief trick to making good mistakes is not to hide them—especially not from yourself. Instead of turning away in denial when you make a mistake, you should become a connoisseur of your own mistakes, turning them over in your mind as if they were works of art, which in a way they are. . . . The trick is to take advantage of the particular details of the mess you've made, so that your next attempt will be informed by it and not just another blind stab in the dark. We have all heard the forlorn refrain "Well, it seemed like a good idea at the time!" This phrase has come to stand for the rueful reflection of an idiot, a sign of stupidity, but in fact we should appreciate it as a pillar of wisdom. Any being, any agent, who can truly say, "Well, it seemed like a good idea at the time!" is standing on the threshold of brilliance.*
>
> —DANIEL DENNETT, *Intuition Pumps and Other Tools for Thinking*

The refrain "Well, it seemed like a good idea at the time!" should be one that echoes through your classroom again and again. By carefully and gently examining *good* mistakes as a class, your students will become more and more accustomed to reframing mistakes in this light.

If you think for a moment about your own reflective practices, chances are, you do some reflection with your colleagues, close friends, or partner. Hashing out the "particular details of the mess you've made" (Dennett 2013, 22) can be most productive and comforting in the presence of a supportive, empathetic fellow mess maker. However, reflection is also an extraordinarily individual practice. When you're left alone with your mind, how do you mull over your mistakes and missteps? Are you as calm and helpful as your best friend? Do you see yourself on the threshold of brilliance? We said in the previous chapter that failure is hard, and the truth is, we're often the hardest on ourselves after something goes wrong.

The challenge, then, is to teach your students that when they are reflecting on their mistakes on their own, they can do so in a way that is just as intentional and enlightening as when you reflect as a whole class. We want our students to feel the sadness or frustration of their mistakes—we all need to—but then turn those mistakes over in their minds not with a sense of regret but with a sense of inquiry, a sense of humor, and a sense of hopefulness.

Check in Regularly with the Ecosystem of the Classroom

As we support children's self-reflection work, it is important that they understand that we don't rehash mistakes purely to relive something that's gone wrong. One of the most effective ways for children to understand the power of reflection is to see how it can actually be an agent of change. The big ideas you come to as a class will change the way they see and act in their day-to-day lives. In the weeks following the whole-class conversation described in Chapter 11, Jeff's class discovered time after time that being flexible was more helpful than solely being persistent.

- **Chart:** Record the big idea your class comes to. Have students add sticky notes to the chart as they notice places where the idea has come up again and been proven true. Change the big idea as the class continues to reflect on a growing base of experiences (see Figure 12.3).
- **Role-Play:** Act out times when a big idea changed a child's thinking or actions. Have students be metacognitive by giving voice to their inner dialogue and their thinking process.
- **Reflect:** Talk about your whole-class reflections. Ask your class: "What made the conversations especially powerful? What speaking or listening moves would allow the conversation to run even more smoothly next time?"

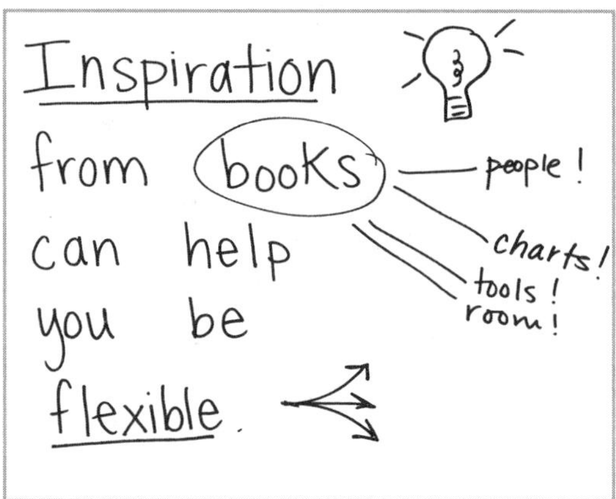

FIGURE 12.3 An Idea That Has Undergone Revision

Check in Regularly with Individual Reflective Practices

Some of the best ways to scaffold children into positive, productive self-reflection can be embedded in the strategies and ideas that we discussed in the preceding chapters. As you work with your students to take on the constellation of stances through self-talk, storytelling, and goal setting, you will find opportunities to weave in strategies for self-reflection.

- **Self-Talk:** Have students think about what type of self-talk helps them when they're thinking over their mistakes and what type of self-talk hurts them. Record these ideas on a chart and refer back to them when you're working with students in small groups or one-on-one conferences.
- **Storytelling:** Help students reframe their mistakes by retelling the stories of what happened. Instead of "I tried to read this word and failed," a child could say, "I tried to read a tricky word and my first strategy didn't work, but I'm the kind of kid who is flexible, so I'm going to try again."
- **Goal Setting:** When goals aren't met, have children reflect on why not. Was the goal too challenging? Not clear enough? Not meaningful enough? Additionally, you can have children set goals to be more reflective and try to come to an aha moment after making a mistake.

In our own lives, creating a time and space for reflection may seem worthwhile but may be hard to actualize. In all aspects of our lives, but especially in our teaching, it is important to slow down as much as we can and celebrate what goes well and reflect on what does not. As we grow more accustomed seeing ourselves "on the threshold of brilliance," our students will reflect this mindset and take their own risks, their own leaps of faith, knowing that we are standing by their side and leaping with them (Dennett 2013, 22).

SUGGESTIONS FOR ENGAGING FAMILIES

- Invite families to create a family reflection time in their week—around the dinner table, in the car, or outside on a walk. Suggest that they talk through something that didn't go quite right and try to think of what they could learn from it.
- Ask parents to talk through their own reflective practices. Suggest that they acknowledge their mistakes and their learning in a positive and gentle way.
- Have families read and reflect on books that celebrate mistakes and growth (see Appendix E for examples).

Closing Thoughts

Teachers have much in common with those special pens that have multiple colors housed within one casing. Click down one side of one of these pens and you'll be writing in red. Click another, and like magic, the pen color will now be blue. Within an educator's core we can call up basic nursing skills, technology skills, the latest in reading and writing research like clicking between colors. Yet, like the colors in those magical pens, all of these skills come together for one purpose: to help the children we see today become the best possible people they can be so that the world of tomorrow will be the best possible world. Teaching without the whole child in our heart and mind is a fruitless enterprise. This book holds our dream for all children: that they grow to be flexible, resilient, empathic, optimistic individuals, brave in the face of risk, kind in the face of challenge, joyful and curious in all things. Thank you for sharing this dream with us.

Books, Books, and More Books

About Building a Positive Classroom Culture

Reflecting Children's Lives: A Handbook for Planning Your Child-Centered Curriculum, by Deb Curtis and Margie Carter

Choice Words: How Our Language Affects Children's Learning, by Peter Johnston

Opening Minds: Using Language to Change Lives, by Peter Johnston

Young Investigators: The Project Approach in the Early Years, by Judy Harris Helm and Lillian Katz

Mindset: The New Psychology of Success, by Carol Dweck

About Play

Play: How It Shapes the Brain, Opens the Imagination, and Invigorates the Soul, by Stuart Brown and Christopher Vaughan

Tools of the Mind: The Vygotskian Approach to Early Childhood Education, by Elena Bodrova and Deborah Leong

A Quick Guide to Boosting English Language Acquisition in Choice Time, K–2, by Alison Porcelli and Cheryl Tyler

About Workshop Teaching

The Art of Teaching Reading, by Lucy Calkins
The Art of Teaching Writing, by Lucy Calkins
Growing Readers: Units of Study in the Primary Classroom, by Kathy Collins
Already Ready: Nurturing Writers in Preschool and Kindergarten, by Katie Wood Ray and Matt Glover

About Building Independence

Smarter Charts, K–2: Optimizing an Instructional Staple to Create Independent Readers and Writers, by Marjorie Martinelli and Kristine Mraz
Smarter Charts for Math, Science, and Social Studies: Making Learning Visible in the Content Areas, by Kristine Mraz and Marjorie Martinelli

About Learning Sequences

Words Their Way: Word Study for Phonics, Vocabulary, and Spelling Instruction, by Donald Bear, Marcia Invernizzi, Shane Templeton, and Francine Johnston
Guided Reading: Good First Teaching for All Children, by Irene Fountas and Gay Su Pinnell
Young Mathematicians at Work series, by Catherine Twomey Fosnot and others
Assessing Writers, by Carl Anderson

About Teachers as Researchers

The Art of Classroom Inquiry: A Handbook for Teacher-Researchers, Ruth Shagoury Hubbard and Brenda Miller Power
Living the Questions: A Guide for Teacher-Researchers, by Ruth Shagoury and Brenda Miller Power

About the Flow of Conferring

How's It Going? A Practical Guide to Conferring with Student Writers, by Carl Anderson
Conferring with Readers: Supporting Each Student's Growth and Independence, by Jen Serravallo and Gravity Goldberg

Note-Taking Form for Whole Class Conversations

Child's Name	Comment/Question	Teacher Noticings
Ex.: *Samira*	Ex.: *"Every time we tried to build our catapult, it would just fall apart."*	Ex.: *Makes eye contact* *Resolves who should talk first*

Kid Watching Form

Questions to Keep in Mind:

- What is this child trying to do?
- What seems easy/hard for this child?
- What stances can you see evidence of? How?

Start/End Activity	What Do You See?	What Do You Hear?	What Do You Notice or Wonder?
Ex.: *9:10–9:15 Writing*	*S writes Fal, crosses out, writes Fil, crosses out, looks around table, scribbles in top left corner, gets up and goes to library, comes back with book—copies "FLASH"*	*/ffffuuuuuhhh/ /fffffffffffulllllllll/*	*Did S know it looked wrong? Is that why he got the book? If we had no Flash superhero book, what would he have done?*

Conferring Sheet with Goals

Ask:

- What are you working on?
- What feels easy? What feels hard?
- How can I help you?

Date/ Name	Child's Comments	Teacher Noticings/Teaching	Goal

Books for Children That Celebrate the Constellation of Stances

Many books celebrate the constellation of stances, but these are the ones we love and turn to again and again.

Book	Stances
Grades K–2	
Bunny Cakes, by Rosemary Wells	Persistence, flexibility, optimism
Elephants Cannot Dance! by Mo Willems	Optimism, persistence
Everyone Can Learn to Ride a Bicycle, by Chris Raschka	Persistence, optimism, resilience
Oh No, George! by Chris Haughton	Resilience
Lily the Unicorn, by Dallas Clayton	Optimism
How to Be a Jedi, by Quinlan B. Lee (from *Star Wars: Phonics* Boxed Set)	Resilience, persistence
Worm Builds, by Kathy Caple	Resilience, persistence, flexibility
Leonardo the Terrible Monster, by Mo Willems	Empathy
The Amazing Spider-Man, by Thomas Macri	Flexibility, resilience
Almost, by Richard Torrey	Optimism, persistence
Big Red Lollipop, by Rukhsana Khan	Empathy
Yo! Yes? by Chris Raschka	Empathy
Grades 3–5	
Rosie Revere, Engineer, by Andrea Beaty	Resilience, persistence, optimism, flexibility
The Most Magnificent Thing, by Ashley Spires	Optimism, flexibility, resilience
A Home for Bird, by Philip Stead	Empathy, persistence
Beautiful Oops! by Barney Saltzberg	Resilience, optimism
Going Places, by Paul Reynolds	Optimism
Those Shoes, by Maribeth Boelts	Empathy
Author: A True Story, by Helen Lester	Persistence, resilience
Freedom Summer, by Deborah Wiles	Empathy
Each Kindness, by Jacqueline Woodson	Empathy
Wilma Unlimited: How Wilma Rudolph Became the World's Fastest Woman, by Kathleen Krull	Persistence, resilience
If You Want to See a Whale, by Julie Fogliano	Persistence, flexibility, resilience, optimism

Works Cited

Alvarez, A. L., and A. E. Booth. 2014. "Motivated by Meaning: Testing the Effect of Knowledge-Infused Rewards on Preschoolers' Persistence." *Child Development* 85 (2): 783–91.

Aschwanden, Christie. 2011. "The Magic of Mantras." *Runner's World*, January 10. www.runnersworld.com/race-training/magic-mantras.

Beck, Isabel. 2013. *Bringing Words to Life: Robust Vocabulary Instruction*. 2nd ed. New York: Guilford.

Blair, Julie. 2014. "Knowledge Motivates Preschoolers More Than Stickers, Study Says." *Education Week: Early Years*, March 25. http://blogs.edweek.org/edweek/early_years/2014/03/knowledge_motivates_preschoolers_more_than_stickers_study_says.html.

Bodrova, Elena, and Deborah Leong. 2007. *Tools of the Mind: The Vygotskian Approach to Early Childhood Education*. Upper Saddle River, NJ: Pearson/Merrill Prentice Hall.

Brown, Brene. 2012. *Daring Greatly: How the Courage to Be Vulnerable Transforms the Way We Live, Love, Parent, and Lead*. New York: Gotham Books.

Bruce, Tina. 1999. "In Praise of Inspired and Inspiring Teachers." In *Early Education Transformed*, edited by Lesley Abbott, 33–40. London: Falmer.

Calkins, Lucy. 1994. *The Art of Teaching Writing*. Portsmouth, NH: Heinemann.

Casebeer, William, and Paul Zak. 2013. "Empathy, Neurochemistry and the Dramatic Arc" (video). *Future of StoryTelling* (blog), May 16. http://futureofstorytelling.org/video/empathy-neurochemistry-and-the-dramatic-arc/.

Catmull, Edwin E., and Amy Wallace. 2014. *Creativity, Inc.: Overcoming the Unseen Forces That Stand in the Way of True Inspiration*. New York: Random House.

Chen, Ingfei. 2014. "How a Bigger Purpose Can Motivate Students to Learn." *MindShift*, August 18. http://ww2.kqed.org/mindshift/2014/08/18/how-a-bigger-purpose-can-motivate-students-to-learn/.

Clay, Marie. 2014. *By Different Paths to Common Outcomes*. Portsmouth, NH: Heinemann.

Costa, Arthur, and Bena Kallick. 2000. *Discovering and Exploring Habits of Mind*. Alexandria, VA: ASCD.

———. 2009. *Learning and Leading with Habits of Mind: 16 Essential Characteristics for Success*. Alexandria, VA: ASCD.

Curtis, Deb, and Margie Carter. 2011. *Reflecting Children's Lives: A Handbook for Planning Your Child-Centered Curriculum*. St. Paul, MN: Redleaf.

Dean, Jeremy. 2013. *Making Habits, Breaking Habits: Why We Do Things, Why We Don't, and How to Make Any Change Stick*. Cambridge, MA: Da Capo Lifelong Books.

Dennett, Daniel. 2013. *Intuition Pumps and Other Tools for Thinking*. New York: W. W. Norton.

Duhigg, Charles. 2014. *The Power of Habit: Why We Do What We Do in Life and Business*. New York: Random House.

Dweck, Carol. 2007. *Mindset: The New Psychology of Success*. New York: Random House.

Foer, Joshua. 2013. "Learning to Live Outside Your Comfort Zone." In *Maximize Your Potential: Grow Your Expertise, Take Bold Risks and Build an Incredible Career*, edited by Jocelyn K. Glei. New York: Amazon.

Fondas, Nanette. 2014. "Study: You Really Can 'Work Smarter, Not Harder.'" *Atlantic*, May 15. www.theatlantic.com/education/archive/2014/05/study-you-really-can-work-smarter-not-harder/370819/.

Fries, Amy. 2010. "Sparking Creativity in the Workplace." *The Power of Daydreaming* (blog), February 9. www.psychologytoday.com/blog/the-power-daydreaming/201002/sparking-creativity-in-the-workplace.

Ginsburg, Kenneth, and Martha Jablow. 2011. *Building Resilience in Children and Teens: Giving Kids Roots and Wings*. Elk Grove Village, IL: American Academy of Pediatrics.

Gordon, Mary. 2005. *Roots of Empathy: Changing the World, Child by Child*. Toronto: Thomas Allen.

Gottschall, Jonathan. 2013. *How Stories Make Us Human*. Boston: Mariner Books.

Halverson, Heidi Grant. 2013. "Focusing on Getting Better Rather Than Being Good." In *Maximize Your Potential: Grow Your Expertise, Take Bold Risks and Build an Incredible Career*, edited by Jocelyn K. Glei. New York: Amazon.

Hamilton, Jon. 2014. "How Play Wires Kids' Brains for Social and Academic Success." *MindShift*, August 7. http://blogs.kqed.org/mindshift/2014/08/how-play-wires-kids-brains-for-social-and-academic-success/.

Hattie, John, and Gregory Yates. 2013. *Visible Learning and the Science of How We Learn*. New York: Routledge.

Hemingway, Ernest. 1957. *A Farewell to Arms*. New York: Charles Scribner's Sons.

Hubbard, Ruth Shagoury, and Brenda Miller Power. 2003. *The Art of Classroom Inquiry*. Portsmouth, NH: Heinemann.

Johnston, Peter. 2004. *Choice Words: How Our Language Affects Children's Learning*. Portland, ME: Stenhouse.

Kohn, Alfie. 2014. "Sometimes It's Better to Quit Than to Prove Your Grit." *The Washington Post*, April 6. Accessed online April 9, 2014. www.washingtonpost.com/opinions/sometimes-its-better-to-quit-than-to-prove-your-grit/2014/04/04/24075a84-b8f8-11e3-96ae-f2c36d2b1245_story.html.

Krechevsky, Mara, Ben Mardell, Melissa Rivard, and Daniel Wilson. 2013. *Visible Learners: Promoting Reggio-Inspired Approaches in All Schools*. San Francisco: Jossey-Bass.

Lewis, Sarah. 2014. *The Rise: Creativity, the Gift of Failure, and the Search for Mastery*. New York: Simon and Schuster.

McFarlin, Dean B., Roy F. Baumeister, and Jim Blascovich. 1984. "On Knowing When to Quit: Task Failure, Self-Esteem, Advice, and Nonproductive Persistence." *Journal of Personality* 52 (2): 138–55.

Miller, Debbie. 2008. *Teaching with Intention*. Portland, ME: Stenhouse.

Perry, Philippa. 2009. *How to Stay Sane*. London: Picador.

Pink, Daniel. 2005. *A Whole New Mind: Moving from the Information Age to the Conceptual Age*. New York: Riverhead Books.

———. 2009. *Drive: The Surprising Truth About What Motivates Us*. New York: Riverhead Books.

Rashcka, Chris. 2013. *Everyone Can Learn to Ride a Bicycle*. New York: Schwartz and Wade Books.

Ros, Hana, and Matteo Farinella. 2013. *Neurocomic*. London: Nobrow.

Rosin, Hanna. 2014. "The Overprotected Kid." *Atlantic*, April. www.theatlantic.com/features/archive/2014/03/hey-parents-leave-those-kids-alone/358631/.

Schwalbe, Michael. 2013. "Demystifying the Fear Factor in Failure." In *Maximize Your Potential: Grow Your Expertise, Take Bold Risks and Build an Incredible Career*, edited by Jocelyn K. Glei. New York: Amazon.

Schwartz, Tony. 2013. "Developing Mastery Through Deliberate Practice." In *Maximize Your Potential: Grow Your Expertise, Take Bold Risks and Build an Incredible Career*, edited by Jocelyn K. Glei. New York: Amazon.

Seligman, Martin. 2006. *Learned Optimism: How to Change Your Mind and Your Life.* New York: Vintage.

Siegel, Daniel, and Tina Payne Bryson. 2012. *The Whole-Brain Child: 12 Revolutionary Strategies to Nurture Your Child's Developing Mind.* New York: Bantam.

Starecheski, Laura. 2014. "Why Saying Is Believing—the Science of Self-Talk." *Shots: Health News from NPR*, October 7. www.npr.org/blogs/health/2014/10/07/353292408/why-saying-is-believing-the-science-of-self-talk.

Tough, Paul. 2012. *How Children Succeed: Grit, Curiosity, and the Hidden Power of Character*. Boston: Houghton Mifflin Harcourt.

Vonnegut, Kurt. 1999. *Mother Night*. New York: Dial Press Trade Paperback.

Wells, Gordon. 2001. *Action, Talk, and Text: Learning and Teaching Through Inquiry*. New York: Teachers College Press.

Willems, Mo. 2005. *Leonardo the Terrible Monster*. New York: Hyperion Books for Children.

Young, Scott H. 2013. "Reprogramming Your Daily Habits." In *Maximize Your Potential: Grow Your Expertise, Take Bold Risks and Build an Incredible Career*, edited by Jocelyn K. Glei, 105–11. New York: Amazon.